FEAST
◇ of ◇
INDIA

RANI

CB

CONTEMPORARY BOOKS

Rani.
Feast of India : a legacy of recipes and fables / Rani.
p.   cm.
Includes index.
ISBN 0-8092-4095-5 (paper) :
1. Cookery, Indic.   I. Title.
TX724.5.I4R36   1991
641.5954—dc20   91-17974
                                                      CIP

Copyright © 1991 by Mahendri Arundale
All rights reserved
Published by Contemporary Books
An imprint of NTC/Contemporary Publishing Company
4255 West Touhy Avenue, Lincolnwood, Illinois 60646-1975
Manufactured in the United States of America
International Standard Book Number: 0-8092-4095-5
18   17   16   15   14   13   12   11   10   9   8   7   6

Contents

To
my mother, Raja Rajeswari,
my sisters, Nalini and Sheela,
my son, Shiva,
and
to
all the curry lovers

Acknowledgments

My grateful thanks to Ciba-Geigy Corporation, Ms. Gina Dingle, Mr. Philip Flagler, and Ms. Shirley Kiefer of the Ciba-Geigy Corporation; Curtis Licensing Corporation and Ms. Judith Lizama of Curtis Licensing Corporation; Norton Simon Museum and Ms. Lori Hunt of Norton Simon Museum; the John Hopkins University Press and Ms. Arlene W. Sullivan of the Johns Hopkins University Press; Government of India Tourist Offices in India, New York, and Los Angeles, and Mr. K. Lakhanpal of Government of India Tourist Office in New York; Tea Board of India, New York, Mr. Bedi and Ms. Sujata Kapoor of Tea Board of India, New York; Martin of Martin Photography; Iyengar Yoga Institute of San Francisco, Mr. B. K. S. Iyengar of Ramamani Iyengar Memorial Yoga Institute in Pune, India, and Iyengar Yoga Institute of San Francisco, and Ms. Pat Layton of the Iyengar Yoga Institute of San Francisco; Ms. Eileen Nauman, medical astrologer; Mr. George Wupperman, Mr. and Mrs. Larry Yamaki, Mr. Jagdish Singh of India Sweet House, Los Angeles; Mr. Bal Mundkur of Ulka Advertising, India; Mr. Raju Pathak of Pathak Spices International;

Mr. Ben Masselink, Dr. Pratapaditya Pal, Mrs. Linda Verity, Mrs. Leanne Monroe, Mrs. Evelyn Overturf, Ms. Betty Rose, Ms. Rose Smith, Mrs. Hildegard Berry, Mrs. Nancy Lovendosky, Mr. Kapoor of Akbar Restaurant; Ms. Pavla Ustinov; Mrs. Shanti Patel, director of publicity, Department of Tourism, New Delhi; Mrs. Mira Mehrish, deputy secretary, Department of Tourism, New Delhi; Mrs. Devaki Nair, director, West Coast Government of India Tourism, Los Angeles; Mr. M. R. S. Krishnan of India Tourism Development Corporation; Mr. and Mrs. Ishwar Prasad, Australia; Mr. Siddharth Sawhney and Col. A. P. Sawhney, New Delhi; Kaviraj Dr. Khazan Chand, Ayurvedacharya, Ayurveda practitioner, New Delhi; Mr. Manjit S. Gill, executive chef, Maurya Sheraton Hotel and Towers, New Delhi; Spices Board of India, American Spice Trade Association; Ms. Louise Erickson of Lewis and Neale, Inc., New York; Mr. Kannan Natarajan of Paru's Indian Vegetarian Restaurant, Los Angeles; Ms. Bethany Lathrop, Mrs. Virginia Jacobs, Mrs. Gloria Lloyd Roberts, Ms. Joanna Evans, Mrs. Bobbi Davis, Mr. John Cameron, Ms. Gail Rudy, Mr. Rajinder K. Jawa of India Sweets and Spices; Mr. Don Jacobs; and Mr. William Waters.

I would like especially to extend my gratitude to Harold A. Lipton, Esq., for his faith in me; Dr. Donald A. Adams, M.D., F.A.C.P. (nephrology, internal medicine, and hypertension), Dr. Edwin P. Hill, M.D. (eye physician and surgeon, ophthalmology), Dr. Wallace C. Marine, M.D. (obstetrics and gynecology), Dr. Amarjit S. Marwah, B.D.S., D.D.S., M.S. (orthodontist, periodontist, and dental surgeon), Dr. Nobuyuki Fukinbara (acupuncture), and Dr. Gail Dubinsky, M.D. (specializing in musculoskeletal pain and disorders, yoga therapist at Iyengar Yoga Institute of San Francisco), all for their professional expertise; Dr. Frank H. Netter, M.D., illustrator of the Ciba Collection of Medical Illustrations, for his striking illustrations; Mr. Leon Schlossberg and Dr. George D. Zuidema, M.D., illustrators of *The Johns Hopkins Atlas of Human Functional*

Anatomy; Mr. Peter Clarke for his exceptional computer skills; Mrs. Kamala Devi Jackson for her support; Mr. W. Barry Grace for his presentation of illustrations; Mr. K. Natarajan, editor of *Photo Flash*, India, for his photographs; Mr. James W. Thornton; Mr. and Mrs. N. C. Jain; Mrs. Suzanne Cloutier Ustinov for her constructive criticisms and suggestions; Ms. Sheela Arundale for all her coordinating efforts in India; my son, Shiva, for his patience; my late father, Sri M. J. Arundale; and last but not least, I give many thanks to my editor, Ms. Linda Gray, for her prompt and unwavering decision to publish *Feast of India* with Contemporary Books.

Rani (photograph by Bethany)

Introduction

I was born and raised in India, and I came to America in the early 1970s with my American husband. The first six months of marriage in a new world were bewildering, and I could not comprehend the depression that overcame me as a result of this "culture shock." Moreover, I could ill afford to lose the 20 pounds that made me appear to be withering away. Fate stepped in and provided me with the opportunity to discover that I was suffering from a severe case of homesickness. Very simply, I missed my mother's cooking.

My husband was invited to conduct a seminar at a university in another city, stay overnight, and return early the next day. I was completely alone in a major American city for the first time. I began to get very hungry during the early part of the day, and it suddenly dawned on me that I could eat anything I wanted.

My mind drifted back to India and reflected on the happy days spent in my mother's kitchen with Shafi, our khansama (chef), who indulged my childish fancy to learn the science and art of Indian cooking. I laughed to myself remembering that Shafi dutifully threatened to quit every

1

Thursday morning for 20 years. My mother, in response, went to the kitchen every Thursday, listened to Shafi's litany of complaints, and dutifully begged him to change his mind, indicating that every member of the family would surely die of malnutrition if he left. Neither my father nor Shafi could ever deny my mother anything when she performed her motherly "act" to protect the health and well-being of her four "defenseless" children. Shafi is an old man today, the children are grown and married, but would you believe that the two of them were still performing that "Thursday ritual" when I visited my mother last year?

I decided to explore stores in neighborhoods predominantly occupied by immigrants, especially Hindus from all parts of India. It was in these out-of-the-way stores that I discovered all of the Old World spices lined up on shelves in huge glass jars. I could barely contain my excitement and enthusiasm as the scents of the spices produced fond memories of home. I bought pounds of everything in sight and rushed home to indulge and fulfill my passionate longing for real Indian cuisine.

Once I was at home in my kitchen, no power on earth could prevent me from preparing a sumptuous banquet. I cooked everything that I could remember. One curry was not enough; I remember preparing at least 15 dishes. Moreover, I ate the foods in the Indian manner, with my fingers, instead of using disinfected knives, forks, and spoons.

Over the next 15 years our home became a haven of Indian cooking, and I was besieged with American friends who practically invited themselves to dinner. Rather than experience bankruptcy feeding the masses, I began writing down simple recipes for my friends, along with advice about different types of spices.

Shortly thereafter, in letters to my mother, I requested her advice about cooking. To my amazement, and probably because she had little else to do at the time, my mother sent me ancient recipes that I had to translate into English. Furthermore, my mother visited the homes of our relatives and friends in India and acquired more recipes for me. Soon the relatives and friends were contacting me for things they wanted from America, and they thanked me by sending additional information. All of the material for this book was acquired in this fashion over 15 years in addition to the many months I spent researching nutrition, spices, and herbs.

You will find that the Indian dishes described in this book are noted for their therapeutic value, because they are major sources of vitamins and minerals needed to preserve human life. Many physicians (my personal dinner companions) point out the medicinal value of these foods. The close friends I have introduced to Indian cuisine complain less about their body aches, indigestion, and similar disorders.

As for me, life has changed since I came to America. I am very proud to say that my "gift of good health" came from a spiritual reawakening through Indian food, because it promotes creativity, life, vitality, strength, health, laughter, joy, and cheerfulness. Because of the abundance of energy I now have, I have also been able to pursue many different creative endeavors, including taking care of my 19-year-old son, selling real estate, writing, and teaching. All this and much more, in addition to working at a full-time job. For me, my creativity and spirituality blend in harmony with my body and soul. My outward life and my inner being respond to each other harmoniously. The fountain of youth was proclaimed in 800 B.C. by the ancient Upanisads (Secret Teachings): "we are what we eat."

Thus I bid you "welcome" to share the joys of good health and nutrition experienced by many in the world of sensuous culinary delights residing within these pages.

Photo: Courtesy of the
Norton Simon Museum

◇ 1 ◇

Cuisines of India

India is like no other country in the world. Even today, among sophisticated and educated people, there are imperfect notions of what India really is.

India is 5,000 years of civilizations, customs, and languages blended together into a great ethnic beehive of diverse humanity. India is alluring, baffling, bewildering, confusing, enchanting, extraordinary, fascinating, poor, rich, and sensuous.

The past 30 centuries are still evident in India's strange customs, taboos, mysterious buildings, voluptuous carvings, and erotic sculptures. The cities and the tombs of opulent emperors and maharajas remain, and famous legends about their beautiful courtesans and concubines that were guarded by hundreds of eunuchs are still repeated.

India is still the world of the ancient Sanskrit-speaking Dravidians of the South, and you can find carvings of the sensuous deva dasis (temple dancers or servants of God) who abandoned themselves to wild, bewitching pleasures of the flesh in exotic temples. India is the land of Brahma, Visnu, and Siva and the great epics like the Sutras and Vedic scriptures. India is still filled with mystics, soothsayers, and astrologers, infinite romance, wisdom, and mathematical genius. India is the homeland of the Great Soul, Mahatma Gandhi, who led India into freedom from the oppression of British rule through passive resistance, nonviolence, and truth. It is here, in India, with an army of volunteers, that the humble Mother Teresa of Calcutta brings love and care to thousands of despairing souls.

India is a marvelous land of timeless wonders, ethereal grandeur, and pageantry. India can hypnotize you, possess you, repel you, and brand your soul.

The Upanisads state "Annam Brahma"—"Food is God," and therefore it must be given the highest veneration. Even today, in many Indian homes, be they meager or affluent, a symbolic offering of food is given to Brahma before every meal.

There is more to Indian cuisine than curry and Major Grey's Curry Powder (which is just about unheard of in many kitchens of India). Indian cooks would be horrified at the thought of using bottled or canned curry powders because they are capable of mixing their own adventurous and creative blends of curry masalas. A good Indian meal can be found in private homes and not particularly in restaurants, because Indians prefer to entertain in their homes. However, many visitors going to India for the first time are bewildered, embarrassed, and at a loss for words at the hospitality, graciousness, and generosity they encounter. This is part of the intrinsic and intimate nature of the subcontinent's cultural heritage.

The cuisines of India are as mixed as its culture, racial structure, and geography. Characteristic of all Indian cooking, however, is the blending of spices. Apart from being used for flavor, spices stimulate and aid in digestion. Great care is taken not only to ensure that spices enhance rather than dominate the basic flavor of the meal but also to retain their innate nutritional and therapeutic value.

Over the centuries, in the East, eating and conversation have developed into cultivated arts. The people in the East seem to be friendlier and on better terms with their stomachs than people in the West. The aim is not to devour food but to taste it, savor it, and enjoy it because food has a stronger psychological bearing on health than most of us realize. Based on sensible beliefs that developed during the period of the Vedas (knowledge) more than 3,000 years ago, and over centuries of study, testing, and observation, nourishment of the body and contentment of the mind proved vital to the eating habits of the people of the Indian subcontinent. The precepts of the six rasas, or flavors, developed and became part of every meal. Each flavor is believed to have its therapeutic health remedy and was prescribed in a particular proportion to the others. Since food was believed to influence behavior as well as physical well-being, these beliefs were taken very seriously, evolving through time. Today it is an important function of the Indian subcontinent's consciousness, and for this very reason Indians treat their bodies like temples—with gentle and deserved respect.

The dining table or the dining area floor in most homes in India is set with stainless-steel thalis, or plates. In the center of the thali a small portion of steaming hot rice and pappadams accompanies small katoras, or matching stainless-steel bowls filled with different dishes of meat, fish, or chicken, vegetables, legumes, yogurt or curds, and chutneys. During elaborate marriage celebrations in Madras we always sat on the floor on dhurries (carpets) and ate from fresh disposable banana leaves instead of thalis. Most Indians, whether poor or rich, have been conditioned from an early age to eat with the tips of their right fingers. Without the interference of eating utensils, food simply tastes better. Quite honestly, many share my sentiments that eating with knives and forks gives the illusion of making love through an interpreter.

With the foreign and Muslim invasions of India new motifs of living, habits, and tastes and a new cuisine emerged in which meat constituted an important part of the diet in North and Central India. The major Muslim contribution was the tandoor, the clay oven from which emerged a delectable array of kababs (small pieces of meat or seafood seasoned with aromatic spices and herbs, then broiled or fried) and rotis (breads made with whole wheat flour). This was the origin of the famous tandoori cooking, identified with the North but available all over India—tandoori chicken, seekh kabab (made with ground lamb or beef), boti (cubes of lamb, beef, chicken, or fish) and barra kababs (thin strips of lamb or beef), and tandoori fish. Among the rotis are tandoori paratha (baked bread that is lightly brushed with butter) and roomali roti (a bread so thin as to be compared to a muslin kerchief known to go through a slender lady's ring). In contrast the people of the South, for the most part, are staunch vegetarians because of their religious and orthodox conventions and also because they were less affected by foreign invasions.

Milk and milk products are important ingredients in Indian cooking, especially the use of ghee (clarified butter) and dahi (yogurt or curd). Yogurt is considered an excellent meat tenderizer and forms an important part of many recipes. In the North it is seasoned with subtle spices and served with vegetables to create the raitas (yogurt-based salads); in the South it is the base of the coconut pachadis (chutneys). Rice is the staple crop in southern, central, and eastern India and is also eaten in the North as an important accompaniment to meals.

Several varieties of protein-rich legumes, or dals, are grown all over India and are used to make a bewildering variety of dishes, ranging from the sumptuous South Indian sambar and the sweet dals of western India to the delectable ma-ki-dal of the North. Vegetables are seasonal and vary with region.

The vegetarian cuisine of India is extremely varied and evolved over the centuries because of Hindu dogma that all life is sacred and must not be injured. Today, for millions of Indians, purity of mind and spirit demands that they maintain a diet of strict vegetarianism.

The North Indian vegetarian cuisine is called the Benaresi (of Benares) variety. Lightly seasoned, many of its specialties include paneer (cottage cheese), which is a protein-rich substitute for meat. Different varieties of deep-fried pooris and parathas (stuffed breads) are made from wheat, gram, and whole-meal flour. Chapati is the most widely eaten wheat bread in homes all over India.

Seafood is very popular on the South, West, and East Coasts of India. There are endless varieties of fish preparations, and they differ from region to region. The chili-hot Andhra Pradesh fish and prawn curries, the coconut- and curry-flavored Madras prawn and fish curries, the mustard-flavored fish and prawn curries of Bengal, and, of course, the unforgettable fish and shellfish curries of Kerala and Goa are all spectacular.

Seductive Indian sweetmeats and desserts are made from milk and legumes. Famous among them are the North Indian desserts of rasagolla (cream cheese balls in a sweet syrup), sandesh (cream cheese and nut fudges), gulab jaman (milk-flour balls in sweet rose water syrup), barfis (milk fudges), jalebis (pretzel-shaped flour fritters in a sweet syrup), laddoos (sweet gram flour balls), halwas (puddings or sweetmeats), kheer (the Indian equivalent of rice pudding), shahi tukra (an exotic bread pudding), and kulfi (a rich, nutty pistachio and almond ice cream). Desserts and sweets from the South include halwas and the creamy payasam (a milk and crushed cardamom dessert). Halwas are made from carrots, legumes, eggs, semolina, and oatmeal.

After-dinner pan eating continues to be a ritual in India. Pan chewing goes back to before 2000 B.C. Regarded for its digestive and healing properties, pan is an ambrosial mixture of shredded areca nut (betel nut), powdered lime, catechu, shredded coconut, camphor, cardamom, clove, aniseed, and a selection of other exotic ingredients wrapped in a fresh betel leaf. The effect of betel chewing is to reduce hunger, digest meals, and create a sensation of satisfaction and exhilaration.

Every region of India has its individual style of cuisine. Delighting the palate with its masterful use of spices and herbs, India's varied cooking styles are acclaimed throughout the world, not only for their often opulent tastes, but also for the therapeutic and nutritional value of the spices and herbs used in their preparation.

Northern India

From Kashmir on the North to the Deccan in central India, the Mughals exerted their political influence and creative genius. Nowhere is the mystery of these great connoisseurs more evident than in the presence of the timeless wonder of the Taj Mahal and in their remarkable cuisine. The Mughal-influenced cuisine of northern India is distinguished by its nonvegetarian Arab, Persian, and Mughal influences, which include an emphasis on lamb and chicken. Northern Indian cuisine overwhelms one with the delicacy and seductive flavors and textures of its luxurious sauces of dahi, cream, and crushed nuts, and with its succulent lamb and poultry dishes. Today this legacy is widely admired throughout India and the rest of the world.

Southern India

Ancient Tamil Nadu, Kerala, Andhra, Karnataka, and the Deccan, edified by the discovery of gold and precious stones and also by a lucrative foreign trade of spices and silks, were indeed an acclaimed land of prosperity and beautiful banquets. Sangam era (academy of college) poets sang of "succulent chops of meat" and "triple water" (probably coconut milk, palm fruit juice, and sugarcane juice) drunk with burning "toddy" (the intoxicating fermented beverage of the palmyra palm) at the royal feasts that lasted for weeks.

The cuisine of the South is much simpler than that of the North, primarily because South India has remained relatively free from foreign influences and foreign cuisines. Vegetarian dishes are a mainstay here. In no other part of the world are curry and rice inseparable as they are in South India. Rice is the staple food of this region and is the basis of every meal. The largely nongreasy roasted and steamed food of the South is very light, and rice is eaten for breakfast, lunch, tea, and dinner. Mixed with ghee, rice is served with sambar, rasam (a thin peppery soup), vegetables, and pachadi. Coconut is also extravagantly used, in fish, meat, and vegetable curries as well as chutneys.

To the people of India's Southwest Coast, seafood is daily fare. Fishing is a way of life on the Kerala coast, where the best seafood in India is available. Kerala's cuisine is memorable for its seafood, delicately flavored with fresh coconut, Malabar pepper, turmeric, and coriander.

Eastern India

The cuisine of this region is simple and often highly seasoned. Fresh river fish from the Ganges delta is used to create an amazing variety of tempting dishes—fried crispy, cooked in yogurt sauce, or prepared in a masala (spice paste). Pomfret, or betki fish, is famous in Bengal. There are ample rice dishes cooked in aromatic herbs, delicately flavored with legumes and pieces of mutton or seafood. The curries of eastern India are delightfully pungent and highly spiced. The array of traditional Bengali sweets such as rasagollas (a cream cheese dessert in a rich sweet syrup) and sandesh (a yogurt or concentrated milk confection sprinkled with pistachios, cashews, and other nuts) are smooth, rich, and soothing.

Western India

Traditional western Indian cuisine is light. In this part of India cuisine changes with the season, each having its own specialty. Dhansak is a specialty of the Parsi community in western India. It is lamb or chicken cooked with curried legumes and served with steaming white rice. Goan seafood is plentiful and delicious—shrimp, crab, lobster, oyster, and pomfret. Pork vindaloo, marinated in vinegar and mustard, is well known all over the world. Goa is also famous for its brew, feni. Made from either cashew fruit or coconut, it makes a robust drink.

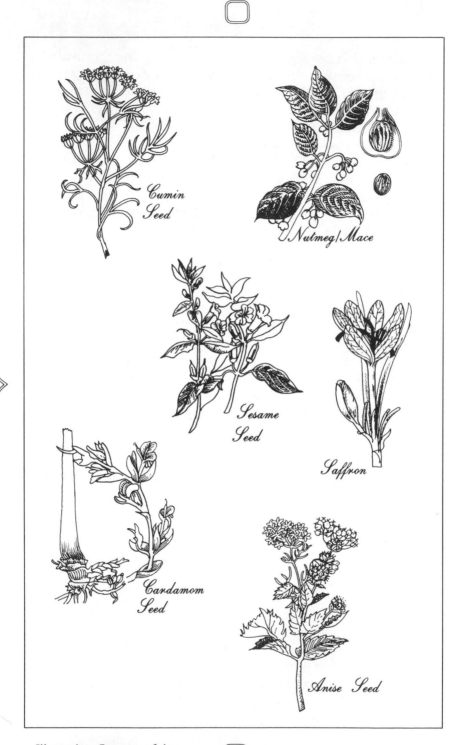

Cumin Seed

Nutmeg/Mace

Sesame Seed

Saffron

Cardamom Seed

Anise Seed

Illustration: Courtesy of the
Spices Board of India

◇ 2 ◇

Spices, Herbs, Oils,
and Legumes Used in
Indian Cooking

Spices, Herbs, and Other Flavorings

The fame of Indian spices is older than recorded history. Centuries before Greece and Rome had their birth, sailing ships carried Indian spices, perfumes, and silks to Mesopotamia, Arabia, and Egypt. It was the lure of these exotic products that brought many seafarers to the shores of India. Long before the birth of Jesus Christ, Greek merchants thronged the markets of South India, buying spices among other precious things. Epicurean Rome spent fortunes on Indian spices, gems, silks, and brocades. The Parthian Wars are believed to have been fought by Rome largely to keep open the trade route to India. In 1492 Christopher Columbus discovered the "New World." Five years later four tiny ships sailed southward from the port of Lisbon, Portugal, under the command of Vasco da Gama. Like Columbus, da Gama was searching for a new route to the spice lands of Asia. While Columbus failed, da Gama succeeded. In a two-year, 24,000-mile round-trip he took his ships around the continent of Africa to India and back to Lisbon. Only two of

13

the four ships survived to reach their home port. These two ships brought back a cargo of spices and other products worth 60 times the cost of the voyage. Vasco da Gama's successful voyage intensified an international power struggle for control over the spice trade. For three centuries the nations of Western Europe—Portugal, Spain, France, Holland, and Great Britain—waged bloody sea wars over the spice-producing colonies.

The spices of the East were valuable in Vasco da Gama's time, as they had been for centuries because they could be used to stretch Europe's inadequate supply of food. Spices could be used to preserve meat for a year or more. During the Middle Ages a pound of ginger was worth a sheep, a pound of mace worth three sheep or half a cow. Pepper, the most coveted spice of all, was counted in individual peppercorns, and a sack of pepper was said to be worth a man's life!

Throughout history spices and herbs have been essential in the preparation of foods. In addition to lending flavor to otherwise bland meals, however, many spices and herbs possess medicinal properties that have a profound impact on human health because they affect many of the body's metabolic processes. Almost all of the herbs and spices found in the world are used in the 3,000-year-old Indian medical system of Ayurveda (science of life). Unlike conventional Western medicine, which tends to treat the disease rather than the patient, the system of Ayurveda medicine treats and heals the whole person—physically, psychologically, and spiritually. Spices and herbs play an important role in this holistic treatment method.

The following spices and herbs are used in the recipes in this book and are available at any Indian grocery store and most supermarkets.

Allspice (pimenta) is available whole or ground and is used to flavor vegetables, curry powder blends, pickles, and sweetmeats. A combination of clove, cinnamon, nutmeg, and black pepper, allspice is used in Ayurveda medicine to aid digestion.

Almonds (badam) are used frequently to garnish pilao, biryani, korma, and curry dishes.

Aniseeds or **fennel seeds** (sounf) have a licorice flavor and are used widely in Kashmiri cuisine. Aniseed is also served after meals as an aid to digestion.

Asafoetida (hing) is a pale yellow to dark brown dried gum resin generally found in Indian markets. Sold in pieces or in ground form, it is most definitely an acquired taste and is used to season seafoods and legume (dal) dishes. Because of its pungent flavor only a pinch is usually added to hot oil and allowed to sizzle for just a few seconds before the other ingredients are added. In India, asafoetida is used in the treatment of asthma and rheumatism.

Bay leaves (tej patha) are used to flavor pilao, biryani, curry, and kabab dishes. Bay leaves are one of the five important spices (cardamom, cinnamon, cloves, and peppercorns being the other four) used to give pilao and biryani dishes their distinctive delicate fragrance and flavor. Bay leaves are also one of several ingredients used in making curry powder.

Besan (chick-pea flour) is used to make pakoras, to flavor shami and seekh kababs, and also to thicken curry sauce/gravy. It is exceptionally rich in protein.

Black cumin seeds (shah jira, zeera, or kala jira/zeera) resemble caraway seeds and are a smaller, delicate, sweeter-smelling, and darker variety than cumin seeds. Black cumin is used whole and does not require roasting; it is an important ingredient in Kashmiri- and Mughalai-style cooking.

Black salt (kala namak) is a rock salt with a distinctive flavor. It is dark brown in color and available in powdered form and is an important ingredient in northern Indian–style appetizers (alu-chat) and sweet and sour chutneys.

Caraway seeds (shia jira) are used to flavor breads, pickles, and vegetables.

Cardamom pods (elaichi) come in two different varieties—small and green, and black (kala elaichi). In the United States, green cardamom pods are bleached to a whitish color. Pods are used whole to flavor pilao, biryani, korma, kabab, and curry dishes, while ground cardamom is an important ingredient in curry powder. Ground cardamom is also used in flavoring puddings and sweetmeats. In India, cardamom seeds are chewed after dinner (along with shredded nutmeg and whole cloves) to aid digestion and to freshen the palate.

Carom or **lovage** (ajowan) resembles celery seeds and has a piquant taste. It is used whole, to flavor vegetable dishes, breads, some northern Indian–style fish preparations, and several varieties of pickles.

Cashew nuts (kaju) are used primarily to flavor Mughal dishes such as biryani, korma, pilao, and curries and to make cashew fudge (kaju barfi). Indian cooking employs raw, not toasted, cashews. Raw cashews may be purchased at health food stores as well as Indian markets.

Chilies, dried red (lal mirchi) enhance the flavor of a curry. These are used whole as well as in crushed and powdered forms. In recipes calling for powdered red chilies, cayenne may be substituted if necessary. Use caution when handling red chilies, as they can burn your skin as well as your mouth.

Chilies, fresh green (hari mirchi) are an important ingredient in Indian cooking and are used in almost all chutneys, vegetable snacks, and curry, vegetable, and legume dishes. Although the seeds of chilies may be discarded before using the meat of the pepper in cooking, they add an enormous amount of flavor (as well as bite) to dishes.

Cilantro (hara dhaniya patha) is available in all supermarkets and Indian grocery stores. It is also known as Chinese parsley or fresh coriander and is used to garnish curries and vegetable dishes.

Cinnamon (dalchini) is available in sticks and in ground form. It is one of the five essential ingredients (bayleaf, cardamom, clove, and peppercorn being the other four) used in flavoring pilao, biryani, korma, kabab, and curry dishes. Cinnamon is also one of several ingredients used in making curry powder and garam-masala.

Cloves (laung/lavangam) are available in whole or

ground form and are one of the five essential ingredients (bay leaf, cardamom, cinnamon, and peppercorn being the other four) used in flavoring pilao, biryani, korma, kabab, and curry dishes. Clove is also one of several ingredients used in making curry powder and garam-masala.

Coconut (nariyal, copra) is an important ingredient in the preparation of South Indian curries, vegetable dishes, chutneys, and sweetmeats. Coconut is available fresh, in the form of dried flakes, or canned in the form of cream of coconut milk. Coconut milk is a common ingredient in Indian dishes, as well as the liquid from whole fresh coconuts.

Coriander seeds (dhaniya) are available whole or ground and are used a great deal in vegetable and meat dishes. Coriander seeds are one of several ingredients used in the preparation of curry powder and garam-masala. Roasted ground coriander is used frequently to flavor yogurt salads (raitas).

Cumin seeds (jira) are very much like caraway seeds in appearance but have a distinct flavor and come whole or ground. Whole seeds are added to hot oil to flavor vegetable and rice dishes. Many northern Indian recipes use roasted ground cumin to flavor yogurt salads (raitas).

Curry leaves (kari patha) are similar to bay leaves but much smaller and are available fresh or dried. Curry leaves have a distinct aroma and are used to flavor rice, curry dishes, South Indian dishes, and chutneys.

Curry powder (kari masala) is a blend of several spices (ground turmeric, ground dried red chilies, coriander seeds, black pepper, cumin seeds, fenugreek seeds, curry leaves, mustard seeds, cinnamon, cardamom, cloves, nutmeg, peppercorns, and bay leaves), which are ground to a fine paste with onion, garlic, and fresh gingerroot. There are several blends of curry powders, and the ingredients vary with each regional blend in the North, South, East, and West of India.

Fenugreek seeds (methi) are a pale mustard color and have a bitter taste. They are available whole or ground and are used to flavor South Indian dal and vegetable dishes and pickles; they are also an ingredient in South Indian curry powders. In India fenugreek leaves are used as a vegetable.

Flower essences (ruh) are concentrated flavorings used to flavor Mughal-style dishes. Flower essences are available at Indian markets as well as some health food stores.

Garam-masala (hot spice) is a powdered blend of dried spices—cloves, cardamom, cinnamon, black peppercorns, nutmeg, cumin seeds, and coriander seeds.

Garlic (lahsun) plays a very important role in Indian cooking. It is one of the three major seasonings (gingerroot and onion being the other two) used in almost every regional curry, legume (dal), and vegetable dish. Garlic is used extensively in Ayurveda medicine as a treatment for numerous maladies.

Ginger (adrak) also plays a very important role in Indian cooking. Like garlic and onion, it is one of the three major seasonings used in almost every curry, legume, and vegetable dish. Ground ginger is almost never used in Indian cooking. Unless otherwise stated, all of the recipes in this book call for fresh ginger. Peel the skin before using fresh gingerroot.

Jaggery or **palm sugar** (gur) is the sap of coconut palm and palmyra palm and is used in chutneys, sweets, and some vegetable dishes. It is like molasses and is available at Indian markets.

Khus (sandal/khus) is used as an extract to flavor many desserts, beverages, and other dishes. It is available as an essence in Indian markets and in some health food stores.

Mace (javitri and jaiphal) is available whole or ground. It is used to season curries, biryanis, kormas, and desserts.

Mango powder (amchur) is a sour powder made from drying the flesh of green mangoes and is used in some vegetable dishes and chutneys to add a piquant flavor. It is available at Indian markets.

Mint leaves (pudina patha) are used in curries, biryanis, kormas, and chutneys.

Mustard seeds (rai) come in three varieties—yellow, brown, and black—and are available whole or ground.

Whole black mustard seeds are the most commonly used in Indian cooking. They are generally sautéed in hot oil to give flavor to vegetable and legume dishes and chutneys. Ground mustard seeds are used in some curry blends and seafood dishes. If ground mustard seeds are not available, dry mustard may be substituted. In northern India mustard oil is used for pickling vegetables. In India mustard leaves are eaten as a vegetable.

Nutmeg (jaiphal) is used in South Indian curries, in garam-masala, and to flavor sweetmeats.

Onion seeds (kalonji), also known as nigella, have nothing to do with the onion family except that they do resemble actual onion seeds. The black seeds are similar in size and shape to sesame seeds and are used as a pickling spice and to flavor vegetable dishes or are sprinkled over nan (bread).

Onions (pyaz) are used in practically every dish; they are also pickled or eaten raw. Like garlic and ginger, onions are an important ingredient in curries and determine the consistency of the curry sauce. Generally they are ground with other spices or sautéed in oil. In India, onions are often used to treat circulatory disorders.

Panch phora (in Hindustani *panch* means "five") is a mixture or combination of five different aromatic spices—black mustard seeds, black cumin seeds, black onion seeds, fenugreek seeds, and fennel seeds—used to flavor legume and vegetable dishes.

Paprika (deghi mirchi) is used primarily as a food coloring in tandoori dishes and curry sauces and is also used widely in Kashmiri cuisine in the preparation of meat curries, koftas, and kababs.

Peppercorns, black (kali mirchi) are used whole, coarsely crushed, and ground to season curries, pilaos, vegetables, and other dishes.

Pistachio nuts (pista) are used to garnish desserts. Indian cooking employs unsalted pistachio nuts, which are available in health food stores.

Pomegranate seeds (anardana) are available in both dried and powdered form in Indian grocery stores. They have a piquant taste, and many cooks in northern India use them in vegetable and legume dishes. They give flavor to the filling in vegetable samosas, pakoras, and yogurt salads (raitas).

Poppy seeds (khus khus) are tiny white round seeds available whole in Indian grocery stores. They are used primarily in northern Indian-style cooking to flavor meat and seafood dishes and are sometimes used as a thickening agent.

Rose water (gulab) is the diluted form of rose essence. It is a liquid flavoring distilled from fresh rose petals and is used to flavor desserts, biryanis, and yogurt drinks (lhassis).

Saffron (kesar or zafran) is used to color and flavor pilao, biryani, and curry dishes and desserts and is available in thread or powdered form. It is a most expensive spice, but ¼ teaspoon is more than enough to flavor a pound of meat or a cup of uncooked rice. The best way to use saffron is to soak the threads in hot milk for about 15 minutes prior to using.

Salt (namak) comes in three varieties—black salt, rock salt, and white (table) salt. All three are used in Indian cooking as a spice to flavor food and chutneys; however, in all of these recipes, white (table) salt may be used.

Sandalwood (sandal/khus) is used as an extract to flavor desserts, beverages, and other dishes. It is available as an essence in Indian markets and in some health food stores.

Sesame seeds (til) are tiny beige seeds with a nutty flavor. They are generally roasted and then ground into a paste to flavor curries, rice dishes, desserts, pickles, and chutneys.

Tamarind (imli) is available in pulp, cake, or concentrate form at all Indian grocery stores. To extract the juice from tamarind, soak a piece of tamarind cake in boiling water for about 20 to 30 minutes. Mix and squeeze the cake with water and strain the liquid. Tamarind is used extensively in southern India as a souring agent in the preparation of legumes, vegetable dishes, and chutneys.

Turmeric (haldi) is available in ground form in supermarkets and Indian grocery stores and is used extensively in Indian cooking both to color and to flavor legume, vegetable, curry, and seafood dishes. To the Hindus turmeric is a sacred spice used in every religious ceremony. The mangal sutra, or sacred marriage thread, that is tied around the bride's neck by her husband-to-be is dipped in turmeric paste to ensure an auspicious start for the newlyweds.

Vinegar (sirka) is used to flavor South Indian curries and Portuguese-style vindaloo dishes and pickles. Unless otherwise noted, cider vinegar may be used in all of these recipes.

Oils

In India several types of oils are used in cooking. The following are available at supermarkets and Indian grocery stores. Today, because of the danger in cholesterol, many people use vegetable cooking oils as well.

Coconut oil (narial ka tel) has a delicate flavor and is used mostly in Kerala.

Ghee (clarified butter) is used extensively in Indian cooking. It is available at Indian grocery stores, or you can make it yourself. Melt two sticks of unsalted butter in a saucepan and let the butter simmer until it starts turning golden brown. Stir for 30 minutes or until the liquid evaporates and remove the pan from the heat. Strain through a cheesecloth, cool, and refrigerate.

Mustard oil (sarson ka tel) has a strong aroma and is used mainly in northern India. In Bengal fish and vegetable dishes are prepared in mustard oil. Because of its preservative qualities, Portuguese (Goanese) cooking uses mustard oil in its famous vindaloo dishes and seafood pickles.

Peanut oil (momphali ka tel) is used widely in western and southern India.

Sesame seed oil (til ka tel) is used mainly in southern and western India. Both the light and dark versions of this oil are used in Indian cooking.

Legumes (Dals)

There are several varieties of legumes, and they form the mainstay of the diet on the subcontinent of India. Also called *dals*, they are considered to be very healthful and nutritive, and are extremely rich in protein and potassium. In India legumes are available both as fresh vegetables and as dried peas, beans, or lentils.

All of the recipes in this book call for dried legumes. Always wash legumes four or five times under cold running water prior to cooking. Some varieties of legumes should be soaked overnight to tenderize and save cooking time, as indicated in the recipes.

The following legumes are available at Indian grocery stores, and most of them can be found at your local supermarkets.

Black gram or **black chick-peas** (kala chana) are a smaller variety than the chole and should be soaked in water prior to cooking. They are used widely in Rajasthan and western India.

Black-eyed peas or **cowpeas** (lobia) are white kidney-shaped beans with a black "eye." This variety of legume is popular in North India, South America, and Africa.

Chick-peas or **garbanzos** (chole or kabuli chana) should be soaked in water overnight to tenderize them and reduce the cooking time. These legumes are used widely in Middle Eastern and South American cuisine as well. Middle Eastern hummus, for example, is made from the garbanzo.

Pigeon peas (arhar dal or toovar dal) are small yellow split peas used predominantly in South India.

Pink lentils (masoor dal) are small and salmon-colored and take less than 20 minutes to cook.

Red kidney beans (raajma) are large dark kidney-shaped beans. They should be soaked in water overnight to tenderize them and reduce the cooking time. This variety of legume is very popular in Punjabi and Rajasthani cuisines.

Red mung beans (mowth dal) are particularly popular in Rajasthan and Gujarat.

Round green or **yellow split peas** (matar dal) are excellent for soups and lentil curries. However, they do need to be soaked for an hour prior to cooking.

Split black beans or **gram** (urid dal) are pale cream in color and cook to a thick consistency. This variety is very popular in South Indian cuisine.

Split yellow mung lentils (moong dal) are split mung beans. In India this variety is served to invalids and babies.

Whole black beans (ma-ki-dal) are a favorite in the Punjab and the frontier country. They are usually cooked with abundant ginger and spices and served with fresh chapatis.

Whole mung beans (saboot moong dal) are the beans that produce the very popular bean sprouts used in salads and Oriental dishes.

Yellow split peas, also known as split chick-peas or garbanzos (chana dal) are the most widely used dal. The gram flour, or besan, is used to make pakoras (hors d'oeuvres) and is versatile as a sauce thickener.

Photo: Courtesy of the
Norton Simon Museum

◇ 3 ◇

Cooking Techniques of India

The preparation of Indian foods is not as complicated as most people make it out to be. All you need to do is follow the basic techniques, and even the most hard-to-understand recipe becomes quite simple to prepare. Just remember not to substitute spices, because the flavor of the dish will change. Whole spices retain flavor longer than ground ones. Use a spice or coffee grinder to make your dry garam-masala (spice blends) and curry powder blends and use an electric blender to grind your wet masala. I also use a mortar and pestle, a kitchen mallet, and a rolling pin, which I find handy for grinding small quantities of roasted cumin, coriander, fennel seeds, asafoetida, peppercorns, cloves, and cardamom seeds.

In the South masalas are ground with a liquid (coconut milk, water, lime juice, or vinegar) to make a paste, while in the North dry spices are used much more frequently.

The real secret of spicing and seasoning foods is not only which spices you use but also *how* you use them. In time you will develop a better understanding of the relationships among aromas, flavors, and textures. Your trained

25

palate should never be able to taste any particular spice you
have used. Most important of all, there should never be a
raw (kacha) taste to a dish (the curry masala should always
be sautéed and cooked thoroughly in oil or ghee before the
meat or vegetables are added). A dish is considered well
cooked when the spices blend into the curry sauce or gravy
and the meat or vegetables.

In India most cooks do not use any system of weighing
or measuring cooking ingredients. They rely solely on what
they have learned by trial and error, by what they have been
taught, or by what is passed down from generation to generation. Some seasoned chefs can merely look at vegetables,
meat, and spices and tell you precisely how much they weigh.
Like my mother and Shafi, their eyes and hands, instincts
and judgment have guided and helped them over the years in
using just the right proportions in the preparation of their
dishes. There are no hard and fast rules for the preparation
of any one particular dish, because the ingredients may be
the same but the quantities will always vary. Therefore, my
advice is to use plain common sense and your instincts in
the preparation of Indian cuisine. Practice makes perfect.

The following cooking techniques are often used in Indian
cooking.

Roasting Dry Spices

Garam-masala, ground cumin and coriander, whole cumin
and coriander seeds, and whole curry spices are roasted dry
in a frying pan or an iron griddle over medium heat. Preheat
the pan and stir the spices with a wooden spatula until the
spices turn a shade or two darker (approximately two to
three minutes). You will know the spices have been roasted
when their aroma fills your kitchen. Whole spices generally
take longer to roast than powdered ones. Let the roasted
spices cool for a few minutes and then grind them in a spice
or coffee grinder.

Grinding Masalas

A spice or coffee grinder is useful for powdering garam-masala and curry powder blends. If you decide to make extra, store it in airtight jars in a dry place so the fragrance of the spices is not lost. The use of a blender proves indispensable for grinding fresh curry masalas.

As a child, I was absolutely fascinated by a ritual that took place almost every month in my parents' home in Lucknow. A group of professional masala pounders made up of three or four women would arrive at the beginning of every month with their heavy pounding and grinding equipment to pound a month's supply of masalas for my mother. The same ladies would also clean rice, wheat, flour, and legumes for my mother.

Seasoning Dals (Baghar or Tarka)

In a small pan, heat some oil or ghee and add the required amount of cumin and mustard seeds, chopped onion or garlic, crushed dried red chilies, and a pinch of asafoetida. Stir and cook for a minute, removing the pan from the heat when the mustard seeds start popping. This blend of seasonings is used to garnish cooked lentils served with rice or chapatis.

Browning Onions, Garlic, Ginger, and Chilies

There are basically two methods for browning these ingredients: (1) chopping or slicing the ingredients and frying them in oil or ghee until they are golden brown and (2) chopping, blending them to a paste (masala), and then sautéing this masala in oil.

Frying Spices and Wet Masala

This is one of the key secrets to flavoring a dish, because this process actually removes the raw taste of the spices. The flavor of fried spices more thoroughly penetrates meat and vegetables than if the spices were boiled in water or coconut liquid. Heat the oil over medium heat to 350°F. (To test the temperature of the oil, add a drop of water to it. If the water sizzles, the oil is hot enough.) Reduce the heat to low before adding spices. As a general rule, frying whole spices takes a minute or two longer than frying ground spices. Just make sure that the spices do not burn. Please note: when mustard seeds are being fried, it is very important that the seeds pop to bring flavor to the dish. When this begins to happen, cover the pan or pot. Unpopped seeds are bitter and pungent. When frying cumin seeds, make sure the seeds turn golden brown and emit their aroma before adding the other ingredients.

It is also important to know how to fry wet masala for a curry. The oil must always be preheated and the masala added, cooked, and thoroughly stirred. Cover and cook for two or three minutes; stir again. Repeat this process two or three times, until the masala is golden brown and the aroma of the spices titillates your nostrils. Make sure the masala does not stick to the pan or pot. Should this happen, add some water and stir again before adding the other ingredients.

Korma or Braising

To braise is to cook meat by browning it in fat and then simmering it in a covered pan with a little liquid. A korma is a thick, rich, and luxurious sauce consisting of delicate spices and herbs, plain yogurt, cream, almonds, and cashews that covers pieces of poultry, lamb, and vegetables. The process of braising in India is quite similar to that of Western cooking, but the meat is marinated in yogurt and spices and then cooked very slowly in the marinade itself over live coals.

Dum or Pot Roasting

The meats must be pricked with a fork or delicately slit on the surface with a knife to allow the spices and seasonings to penetrate. It is important to use a tight-fitting lid. This particular technique uses a fairly large amount of oil or ghee, as the basic ingredients are steamed in it. The spices and seasonings must initially be fried, and the ingredients to be "dum" or pot roasted are added and browned lightly. Increase the heat for a minute; if the ingredients look dry, add a little water. Cover with the lid and turn the heat to low. It is important to check the dum periodically to prevent overcooking. I have found aluminum foil very useful in pot roasting. Simply cover the pot with foil and then cover with the lid, making sure you can remove the foil from time to time to check the ingredients in the pot. Shafi, our family chef, always placed the pot over hot ashes and covered the lid with live charcoal, sealing the pot with a little dough to prevent any steam from escaping. You can replicate this process by placing the pot in a preheated oven (300–350°F) for 20 minutes when you are preparing your Mughal-style biryanis, pilaos, and kormas. The end result will be quite delectable.

Kabab

One of the techniques for preparing meat is kabab style. *Kabab* refers to small chunks, patties, or balls of lamb, beef, and poultry broiled or fried in herbs and seasonings.

Tandoori Cooking

Originally the tandoor oven was used only for baking bread, but today it is used for making whole tandoori chicken, meat and seafood kababs, and nan and roti (breads). I have found that an electric or gas oven and even a charcoal grill quite efficiently perform the task of a tandoor oven. The secret of tandoori cooking is the marinating of meat in yogurt, considered a meat tenderizer, and spices.

◇ 4 ◇
Curry Powders, Masalas, and Pastes

What Is a Curry?

A curry is basically a casserole of beef, chicken, fish, pork, lamb, ground meat, or vegetables cooked in a masala (a combination of several spices in a paste). *Garam-masala* literally means "hot spice," and it is made by roasting and grinding a variety of dried spices to achieve different flavorings. The basic art of Indian cooking lies in the careful blending of different spices to yield subtle variations in the flavor of foods. The khansamas, or chefs, of India have always been true alchemists, capable of mixing myriad spices that intensify the flavors of almost every kind of food.

There are three very simple, yet extremely important, steps to remember when roasting spices for a curry powder, paste, or masala:

1. Constantly stir the spices as they roast to avoid burning them.
2. Spices have roasted once they become a shade darker than their original color.
3. As spices become roasted and change color, they will give out a distinct aroma, and the pan being used will emit light fumes of smoke.

To derive the exact flavoring desired, roast spices over medium heat for four to five minutes—no more, or the spices will burn.

Curry powders and dry masala blends retain their flavor for up to six months when stored in airtight jars. Pastes must be stored in the refrigerator in airtight containers, and they retain their flavor for about one month.

Basic Curry Powder

(Kari Masala)

Makes ¼ cup

1 tablespoon coriander seeds
1 teaspoon cumin seeds
1 teaspoon ground turmeric
½ teaspoon ground dried red
    chilies

In a small, heavy-bottomed frying pan or on an iron griddle, roast all of the ingredients over medium heat, stirring constantly until the spices become a shade darker (4–5 minutes). Remove the pan from the heat and transfer the spices to a spice or coffee grinder. Grind to a fine powder. Store in an airtight jar.

Savory Curry Powder

(Badhiya Kari Masala)

Makes ½ cup

2 tablespoons coriander seeds   1 teaspoon ground ginger
2 teaspoons cumin seeds   3 dried red chilies
1 tablespoon ground turmeric

In a small heavy-bottomed frying pan or on an iron griddle, roast all of the ingredients over medium heat, stirring constantly until the spices become a shade darker (4–5 minutes). Remove the pan from the heat and transfer the spices to a spice or coffee grinder. Grind to a fine powder. Store in an airtight jar.

Hot and Spicy Curry Powder

(Garam Kari Masala)

Makes 1 cup

½ cup coriander seeds   1 tablespoon fenugreek seeds
¼ cup cumin seeds   3 tablespoons ground turmeric
20 dried curry leaves   2 tablespoons black mustard seeds
1 teaspoon black peppercorns   4 dried red chilies

In a small heavy-bottomed frying pan or on an iron griddle, roast all of the ingredients over medium heat, stirring constantly until the spices become a shade darker (4–5 minutes). Remove the pan from the heat and transfer the spices to a spice or coffee grinder. Grind to a fine powder. Store in an airtight jar.

Spicy South Indian Hyderabad-Style Curry Powder

(Garam Hyderabadi Kari Masala)

Makes 1 cup

6 tablespoons coriander seeds
3 tablespoons cumin seeds
3 tablespoons ground turmeric
1 tablespoon fenugreek seeds
2 tablespoons black mustard seeds
20 green cardamom pods, pods
    removed and discarded
2 cinnamon sticks, broken into
    small pieces
5 bay leaves
½ teaspoon whole cloves
¼ teaspoon ground nutmeg
2 tablespoons aniseeds
1 teaspoon black peppercorns
5 dried red chilies
10 dried curry leaves

In a small heavy-bottomed frying pan or on an iron griddle, roast all of the ingredients over medium heat, stirring constantly until the spices become a shade darker (4–5 minutes). Remove the pan from the heat and transfer the spices to a spice or coffee grinder. Grind to a fine powder. Store in an airtight jar.

Basic Garam-Masala

(Garam-Masala)

Makes 1 cup

1 cup black cardamom pods, pods removed and discarded
5 cinnamon sticks, broken into small pieces

¼ cup black peppercorns
¼ cup caraway or cumin seeds
2 tablespoons whole cloves
¼ whole nutmeg, grated

In a small heavy-bottomed frying pan or on an iron griddle, roast all of the ingredients over medium heat, stirring constantly until the spices become a shade darker (4–5 minutes). Remove the pan from the heat and transfer the spices to a spice or coffee grinder. Grind to a fine powder. Store in an airtight jar.

South Indian–Style Garam-Masala

(Dakshini Garam-Masala)

Makes 1½ cups

5 cinnamon sticks, broken into small pieces
1 cup green cardamom pods, pods removed and discarded
¼ cup black cardamom pods, pods removed and discarded

½ cup whole cloves
½ cup black peppercorns
5 dried red chilies
½ whole nutmeg, grated
½ cup cumin seeds
1 cup coriander seeds

In a small heavy-bottomed frying pan or on an iron griddle, roast all of the ingredients over medium heat, stirring constantly until the spices become a shade darker (4–5 minutes). Remove the pan from the heat and transfer the spices to a spice or coffee grinder. Grind to a fine powder. Store in an airtight jar.

Mughal-Style Garam-Masala
(Mughalai Garam-Masala)

Makes 1 cup

1 cup green cardamom pods,
   pods removed and discarded
2 cinnamon sticks, broken into
   small pieces
¼ cup whole cloves
¼ cup black peppercorns
1 tablespoon ground nutmeg

In a small heavy-bottomed frying pan or on an iron griddle, roast all of the ingredients over medium heat, stirring constantly until the spices become a shade darker (4–5 minutes). Remove the pan from the heat and transfer the spices to a spice or coffee grinder. Grind to a fine powder. Store in an airtight jar.

Kashmir-Style Garam-Masala

(Kashmiri Garam-Masala)

Makes 1 cup

1 cup green cardamom pods,
  pods removed and discarded
½ cup black cumin seeds
¼ cup black peppercorns
5 cinnamon sticks, broken into
  small pieces

¼ cup whole cloves
½ whole nutmeg, grated
½ cup aniseeds or fennel seeds

In a small heavy-bottomed frying pan or on an iron griddle, roast all of the ingredients over medium heat, stirring constantly until the spices become a shade darker (4–5 minutes). Remove the pan from the heat and transfer the spices to a spice or coffee grinder. Grind to a fine powder. Store in an airtight jar.

Madras-Style Curry Paste

(Madrasi Garam-Masala)

Makes 2½ cups

1 cup ground coriander
½ cup ground cumin
1 teaspoon ground black pepper
2 tablespoons ground turmeric
1 tablespoon ground black
  mustard seeds
1 teaspoon ground dried red
  chilies

12 cloves garlic, peeled
1 2-inch piece fresh gingerroot,
  peeled and chopped
¼ cup cider vinegar
¾ cup vegetable oil

Place the spices and vinegar in a blender and puree.

In a small heavy-bottomed frying pan or on an iron griddle, heat the oil over medium heat. Add the pureed mixture and fry, stirring constantly, until the oil separates from the spices (5–6 minutes). Discard excess oil and let the paste cool. Store in an airtight jar in the refrigerator.

Fresh Green Curry Paste

(Taja Hare Kari Masala)

Makes ½ cup

6 cloves garlic, peeled
1 1-inch piece fresh gingerroot,
  peeled and chopped
1 cup fresh mint leaves
1 cup cilantro leaves
2 teaspoons ground turmeric
½ teaspoon whole cloves
10 green cardamom pods, pods
  removed and discarded
¼ cup cider vinegar
1 teaspoon fenugreek seeds
½ cup vegetable oil

Place all of the ingredients except the oil in a blender and puree. Heat the oil in a small heavy-bottomed frying pan or on an iron griddle. Add the puree and fry over medium heat, stirring constantly, until the oil separates from the spices (5–6 minutes). Discard excess oil and let the paste cool. Store in an airtight jar in the refrigerator.

◇ 5 ◇

Appetizers, Chutneys, and Relishes

Braised Meatballs in Yogurt
(Dahiwale Kabab)

Serves 8–10

1 cup plain low-fat yogurt
1 large onion, peeled and
  chopped
3 cloves garlic, peeled
1 ½-inch piece fresh gingerroot,
  peeled and chopped
1 fresh green chili
1 teaspoon roasted ground
  coriander
1 teaspoon roasted ground cumin
½ teaspoon ground turmeric
¼ cup fresh mint leaves
2 pounds lean ground beef or
  lamb
¼ cup vegetable oil

In a blender, place yogurt, onion, garlic, ginger, chili, coriander, cumin, turmeric, and mint leaves. Puree to a fine
mixture. Transfer to a large bowl and thoroughly mix with
the meat. Divide into 20 uniformly sized meatballs. Set
aside.

In a large saucepan, heat the oil over medium heat. Gently
place the meatballs in the oil. Cover and cook for 7–10
minutes, until the meatballs are golden brown and crisp.
Turn over, cover, and cook for another 7–10 minutes. Remove the lid and stir until the liquid has evaporated.

Transfer the meatballs to a serving platter. Skewer each
meatball with a toothpick and serve immediately with Sweet
Mint Chutney (see Index) or the chutney of your choice.

Grilled Skewered Meat Kababs
(Boti Kabab)

Serves 6

2 pounds lean boneless lamb or beef, cut into 1-inch cubes
½ cup plain low-fat yogurt
1 medium onion, peeled and chopped
1 1-inch piece fresh gingerroot, peeled and chopped
3 cloves garlic, peeled
1 teaspoon poppy seeds

1 tablespoon coriander seeds
½ teaspoon ground black pepper
1 teaspoon cumin seeds
½ teaspoon ground turmeric
¼ teaspoon ground dried red chilies
Salt to taste
2 tablespoons vegetable oil

Remove and discard any visible fat from the meat. Place the meat in a bowl and set aside. In a blender, place the yogurt, onion, ginger, garlic, poppy seeds, coriander, black pepper, cumin, turmeric, ground chili, and salt. Puree to a fine mixture. Pour the mixture over the meat and marinate in the refrigerator for 1 hour.

Preheat the oven to broil. Thread the meat onto metal skewers and broil about five inches from the heat for 5–7 minutes on each side, basting with vegetable oil from time to time, until the meat is cooked to taste.

Remove the meat from the skewers and place on a serving platter. Skewer each piece with a toothpick and serve hot with Sweet Mint Chutney (see Index).

Cocktail Meatballs

(Chotte Kofta)

Serves 6

Meatballs

2 pounds lean ground lamb or beef
1 teaspoon ground coriander
1 teaspoon ground cumin
½ teaspoon ground dried red chilies

¼ cup plain low-fat yogurt
1 egg
2 tablespoons finely chopped cilantro leaves
Salt to taste

Sauce

2 cups water
6 cloves garlic, peeled
1 1-inch piece fresh gingerroot, peeled and chopped
1 teaspoon ground cumin
1 teaspoon ground coriander
½ teaspoon ground dried red chilies
1 teaspoon paprika

Salt to taste
¼ cup vegetable oil
1 cinnamon stick
6 green cardamom pods
6 cloves
1 large onion, peeled and chopped fine
½ teaspoon ground turmeric
¼ cup plain low-fat yogurt

Prepare the meatballs: Place all of the ingredients for the meatballs in a bowl and mix thoroughly. Make 20 uniformly sized meatballs and set aside.

Prepare the sauce: Place ¼ cup of the water, the garlic, ginger, cumin, coriander, ground chili, paprika, and salt in a blender and puree. Heat the oil in a large saucepan. Add the cinnamon, cardamom, and cloves and fry over medium heat for 5–6 minutes, until the spices turn a shade darker. Add the onion and fry until brown and soft. Stir in the garlic paste and fry for one minute, stirring constantly. Add the turmeric and mix thoroughly for 2-3 minutes. Stir in the yogurt and cook for one minute. Gently add the meatballs and remaining water, stirring thoroughly. Cover and simmer for 20-30 minutes, stirring occasionally to prevent the sauce from sticking to the bottom of the pan. Remove the lid and increase the heat. Cook until the liquid has evaporated.

Gently transfer the meatballs to a warm serving platter. Remove and discard the whole spices from the sauce and pour the sauce over the meatballs. Skewer each meatball with a toothpick and serve immediately with Sweet Mint Chutney (see Index).

Ginger, Cardamom, and Mint Flavored Kababs

(Shami Kabab)

Serves 6

2 pounds lean ground beef or
  lamb
2 large onions, peeled and
  chopped
1 cup yellow split peas
10 black peppercorns
1 1-inch cinnamon stick, broken
  into pieces
6 green cardamom pods
8 cloves
3 bay leaves
1 1-inch piece fresh gingerroot,
  peeled and chopped
3 dried red chilies
3 cups water
1 teaspoon Basic Garam-Masala
  (see Index)
¼ cup fresh mint leaves
Salt to taste
1 egg
¼ cup vegetable oil
¼ cup all-purpose unbleached
  flour

Place all of the ingredients except the egg, oil, and flour in
a large pot and bring to a boil. Reduce the heat and simmer
until the water has evaporated and the meat is tender, stirring occasionally to prevent the ingredients from sticking to

the bottom of the pan. Drain and discard excess liquid and let the mixture cool.

In a food processor or blender, puree the mixture to a thick paste. With a fork, lightly whip the egg and mix it thoroughly into the meat mixture. Divide the mixture into 12 uniformly sized meatballs and flatten each into a 2-inch-thick patty. Lightly coat a griddle or a frying pan with 1 to 2 teaspoons of the vegetable oil. Heat the pan. Coat the meat patties evenly with the flour Gently place the patties on the griddle, in batches if necessary. Fry over medium heat, turning the patties over every 2–3 minutes and brushing with the remaining vegetable oil, until the patties are cooked to a crispy golden brown.

Garnish the patties with raw onion rings, tomato slices, and finely sliced cucumber. Serve hot with Sweet Mint Chutney (see Index) or with chapatis and legumes.

Skewered Cocktail Lamb Kababs
(Tikka Kabab)

Serves 6

2 pounds lean boneless lamb, cut into 1-inch cubes
Juice of ½ small lemon
Salt to taste
¼ cup vegetable oil
2 cups plain low-fat yogurt
1 medium onion, peeled and chopped
2 teaspoons Basic Garam-Masala (see Index)

3 cloves garlic, peeled
1 ½-inch piece fresh gingerroot, peeled and chopped
1 teaspoon paprika
¼ teaspoon ground dried red chilies
⅛ teaspoon ground black pepper

Remove and discard any visible fat from the meat. Transfer the meat to a bowl and mix it with the lemon juice, salt, and vegetable oil.

Place the yogurt, onion, garam-masala, garlic, ginger, paprika, ground chili, and pepper in a blender and puree to a fine paste. Thoroughly mix the pureed mixture into the meat. Cover and marinate overnight in the refrigerator.

Preheat the oven to 500°F.

Thread the meat on metal skewers and place in the oven. Reduce the heat to 350°F. Bake for 7–10 minutes, basting occasionally. Turn over and bake for another 7–10 minutes, until the meat is brown and tender.

Garnish the meat with sliced onion and lemon wedges. Serve hot with Hot Cilantro Relish (see Index). As a side dish to an entrée, serve with parathas and legumes.

Skewered Cocktail Chicken Kababs
(Murgh Tikka)

Serves 6

4 whole chicken breasts
Juice of 1 medium lemon
Salt to taste
1 cup plain low-fat yogurt
¼ cup vegetable oil
4 cloves garlic, peeled and
    crushed
1 1-inch piece fresh gingerroot,
    peeled and grated fine
1 teaspoon ground cumin
¼ teaspoon ground dried red
    chilies
½ teaspoon Basic Garam-Masala
    (see Index)
1 teaspoon paprika

Remove and discard the fat, skin, and bones from the
chicken. Cut the meat into 1-inch pieces and place on a
platter. Squeeze the juice of the lemon over the chicken
pieces and sprinkle them with salt. Marinate for 30 minutes.

Mix together the yogurt and half of the oil. Blend in the
garlic, ginger, cumin, ground chili, garam-masala, and paprika. Pour it over the chicken and marinate overnight in the
refrigerator.

Preheat the oven to 500°F.

Thread the chicken pieces onto metal skewers and bake for
15 minutes. Baste with the marinade and the remaining oil,
turn over, baste the other side, and bake for 15 minutes
more. Remove the chicken from the skewers and serve on a
platter.

Quick Baked Spicy Kababs
(Garam Shami Kabab)

Serves 6

2 pounds lean ground lamb or
  beef
1 medium onion, peeled and
  grated
5 cloves garlic, peeled and grated
1 ½-inch piece fresh gingerroot,
  peeled and grated
1 fresh green chili, grated
½ teaspoon Basic Garam-Masala
  (see Index)
1 egg
¼ teaspoon ground black pepper
½ teaspoon paprika
2 tablespoons chick-pea flour
1 teaspoon finely chopped fresh
  mint leaves
2 tablespoons plain low-fat yogurt
1 tablespoon vegetable oil
Salt to taste
¼ cup vegetable oil

In a bowl, thoroughly mix all of the ingredients except the
vegetable oil. Divide the mixture into 20 uniformly sized
meatballs. Flatten each to a 1-inch-thick patty. Heat a griddle over medium heat and brush 1 teaspoon of the oil over
the surface. Gently place 6 to 7 kababs on the griddle and
brush with a few drops of oil. Cook for 8–10 minutes, until
golden brown and crisp. Turn over, brush evenly with oil,
and cook another 8–10 minutes. Repeat this process until
all of the kababs are cooked. Serve hot with Sweet Mint
Chutney (see Index).

Cocktail Chicken Drumette Kababs
(Chotte Murgh Tikka)

Serves 8-10

3 pounds small chicken
drumettes
Juice of 1 small lemon
3 cloves garlic, peeled
1 ½-inch piece fresh gingerroot,
peeled and chopped
⅛ teaspoon ground black pepper
½ teaspoon Basic Garam-Masala
(see Index)
¼ teaspoon ground dried red
chilies
½ teaspoon paprika
½ teaspoon ground coriander
½ teaspoon ground cumin
2 tablespoons plain low-fat yogurt
1 tablespoon vegetable oil

Remove and discard the skin from the chicken. Transfer the drumettes to a platter. Squeeze the lemon juice over the chicken and set aside. Place all remaining ingredients in a blender and puree to a fine paste. Pour over the chicken legs. Cover, refrigerate, and marinate for 4 hours.

Preheat the oven to 500°F.

Place the drumettes on a flat baking pan and brush with the marinade. Reduce the oven temperature to 300°F, place the chicken in the oven, and bake for 7–10 minutes, basting occasionally. Turn over, baste, and bake for 7–10 minutes, until the legs are brown. Serve hot with the chutney of your choice.

Tandoori-Style Cocktail Shrimp
(Tandoori Jhinga)

Serves 8–10

2 pounds medium shrimps,
  shelled and deveined
Juice of 1 small lemon
Salt to taste
2 cloves garlic, peeled and grated
  fine
1 1-inch piece fresh gingerroot,
  peeled and grated fine
⅛ teaspoon ground black pepper
1 teaspoon paprika
1 teaspoon roasted Basic Garam-
  Masala (see Index)
1 teaspoon roasted ground cumin
1 teaspoon roasted ground
  coriander
1 teaspoon ground turmeric
¼ cup plain low-fat yogurt
5 tablespoons vegetable oil

Wash and dry the shrimps. Transfer them to a platter and sprinkle with lemon juice and salt. Set aside.

Place all remaining ingredients except 4 tablespoons of the oil in a blender and puree to a fine paste. Mix with the shrimps. Cover, refrigerate, and marinate for 1 hour.

In a wok, heat the remaining 4 tablespoons oil. Add the shrimps and marinade. Cook, stirring frequently, over medium heat for 5–7 minutes, until the shrimps are cooked and the oil separates, making a thick sauce. Transfer to a serving platter and serve hot, accompanied by Sweet Mint Chutney (see Index).

Vegetable Fritters
(Sabzi Pakora)

Serves 8-10

Batter

1 large onion, peeled and chopped fine
2 cups chick-pea flour
1 fresh green chili, chopped fine
1 ½-inch piece fresh gingerroot, peeled and chopped fine
1 teaspoon roasted Basic Garam-Masala (see Index)

1 teaspoon roasted ground cumin
¼ cup finely chopped cilantro leaves
2 tablespoons vegetable oil
½ teaspoon baking powder
½ teaspoon ground turmeric
1½ cups water
Salt to taste

Vegetables

2 cups vegetable oil
1 small eggplant, quartered lengthwise and cut into thin crosswise slices
1 large potato, scrubbed, quartered, and sliced
1 medium zucchini, sliced ⅛-inch thick

1 bunch (about ½ pound) fresh spinach, washed and stalks removed

Prepare the batter: In a large bowl, mix all of the batter ingredients until smooth (the consistency of pancake batter). Set aside.

Fry the vegetables: In a wok, heat the oil and reduce the heat to medium. Thoroughly mix the batter and dip the vegetables in one at a time. Gently place them in the wok and fry for 3-4 minutes. Turn over with a steel spatula and fry for 3-4 minutes, until golden brown. Remove the fritters and drain them on paper towels. Repeat this process until all the vegetables have been fried. Serve hot with the chutney of your choice.

Crispy Rice Lentil Wafers
(Pappadam)

Pappadams are thin, crisp disks, either plain or flavored with spices and seasonings such as garlic and black or red crushed pepper. They are available at all Indian grocery stores as well as some supermarkets, premade and ready to cook.

Serves 6

1 cup vegetable oil
12 lentil wafers

Heat the oil in a wok or saucepan. When the oil is hot, gently place 1 lentil wafer at a time in the oil. With a pair of tongs, gently stir for 3–4 seconds, until the pappadam doubles in size. Remove and drain on paper towels. Repeat this process until all of the pappadams have been fried.

South Indian–Style Deep-Fried Bean Savory

(Vadai)

Serves 8-10

½ cup water
1 cup split black beans, soaked in
   cold water for 4 hours
Salt to taste
1 small onion, peeled and
   chopped fine
1 ½-inch piece fresh gingerroot,
   peeled and chopped fine
1 fresh green chili, chopped fine
2 tablespoons finely chopped
   cilantro leaves
1 cup vegetable oil

Place the water, drained beans, and salt in a blender and puree to a fine paste. Transfer the mixture to a bowl. Thoroughly mix in the onion, ginger, chili, and cilantro. Divide the mixture into 20 uniformly sized balls and flatten them slightly.

In a wok, heat the oil over medium heat. Gently drop the patties into the oil and fry, five at a time, for 2-3 minutes. Turn over and fry for 2-3 minutes, until golden brown and crisp. Remove and drain on paper towels. Repeat this process until all the patties have been fried. Serve hot with Fresh South Indian–Style Coconut Chutney (see Index).

Sweet Mint Chutney

(Meethi Pudina ki Chutni)

1 cup fresh mint leaves
1 medium onion, peeled and
  chopped
1 ¼-inch piece fresh gingerroot,
  peeled and chopped
2 medium tomatoes, chopped
4 fresh green chilies or dried red
  chilies

2 tablespoons light brown sugar
1 tablespoon fresh lemon juice *or*
  ¼ teaspoon tamarind
  concentrate
Salt to taste

Remove and discard the stems from the mint leaves. In a
blender, combine the mint leaves and all other ingredients.
Blend to a fine paste. Serve in a small bowl as an accompaniment to Lucknow-Style Lamb Patties (see Index), hors
d'oeuvres, or any meal.

Fresh South Indian–Style Green Chutney

(Thaingai-Kothimeer Pachadi)

½ cup cilantro
1 cup chopped fresh coconut
4 fresh green chilies
1 medium onion, peeled and
  chopped
1 ¼-inch piece fresh gingerroot,
  peeled and chopped

3 cloves garlic, peeled
¼ teaspoon tamarind concentrate
½ cup water
Salt to taste

Remove and discard the stems from the cilantro leaves. Place
all ingredients in a blender and puree to a fine mixture.
Serve in a small bowl as a dip with appetizers or entrées.

Fresh South Indian-Style Coconut Chutney
(Dakshini Thainkai Pachadi)

2 cups chopped fresh coconut
2 cups plain low-fat yogurt
¼ cup water
¼ cup vegetable oil
1 teaspoon black mustard seeds
⅛ teaspoon asafoetida powder
6 dried red chilies
Salt to taste

In a blender, puree the coconut, yogurt, and water to a fine mixture. Set aside.

Heat the oil in a large saucepan. Add the mustard seeds and asafoetida and fry over medium heat until the seeds start popping. Add the chilies and stir for 30 seconds, until they turn a shade darker. Stir in the coconut puree and salt. Bring to a boil and simmer for 2–3 minutes, stirring constantly. Remove from the heat and let cool. Serve with Vegetable Fritters (see Index).

Note: This chutney keeps for 3–4 days in the refrigerator.

Sweet Mango Chutney
(Aam ki Chutni)

6 firm half-ripe mangoes, peeled
   and sliced thin
1 cup cider vinegar
1 cup packed light brown sugar
10 cloves garlic, peeled and
   sliced

1 1-inch piece fresh gingerroot,
   peeled and sliced thin
1 teaspoon ground dried red
   chilies
Salt to taste

Bring all of the ingredients to a boil in a medium-sized pot. Reduce the heat to low and simmer for 30–40 minutes, stirring occasionally to prevent the ingredients from sticking to the bottom of the pan. Remove the pan from the heat and let the chutney cool before serving.

Hot Cilantro Relish
(Hari Dhaniya ki Chutni)

1 cup cilantro
1 medium onion, peeled and
   chopped
2 medium tomatoes, chopped
1 ¼-inch piece fresh gingerroot,
   peeled and chopped

4 fresh green chilies
1 tablespoon fresh lemon juice *or*
   ¼ teaspoon tamarind
   concentrate
¼ cup water
Salt to taste

Remove and discard the stems from the cilantro. Place all of the ingredients in a blender and puree to a fine mixture. Serve in a small bowl as a dip for appetizers and entrées.

Cucumber, Onion, and Tomato Relish

(Kachoombar)

> 1 cup peeled and chopped
>   cucumber
> 1 medium onion, peeled and
>   chopped
> 3 fresh green chilies, sliced fine
> 1 large tomato, chopped
> Juice of 1 small lemon
> ½ teaspoon roasted ground cumin
> ¼ cup chopped cilantro leaves
> ½ cup chopped green bell pepper

Place all ingredients in a mixing bowl. Thoroughly mix together and let stand for 15–20 minutes. Serve with tandoor-style dishes.

Yogurt with Fresh Mint and Eggplant
(Baigan ka Raita)

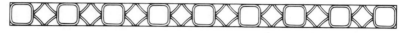

>   1 large eggplant, cut into 1-inch
>   cubes
>   2 cups plain low-fat yogurt
>   ⅛ teaspoon ground dried red
>   chilies
>   ½ teaspoon roasted ground cumin
>   Salt to taste
>   1 tablespoon finely chopped fresh
>   mint leaves
>   1 small onion, peeled and sliced
>   fine
>   1 scallion, sliced fine

Steam the eggplant for 10 minutes. Mash it with a fork and set it aside to cool.

Place the yogurt, chili, cumin, salt, mint, onions, and scallion in a bowl. Mix thoroughly. Stir in the mashed eggplant. Serve chilled with your choice of curry and vegetables.

Yogurt with Potato, Cucumber, and Cilantro

(Alu ka Raita)

Salt to taste
¾ cup peeled and grated cucumber
1 large potato, peeled, boiled, and
  cut into ¼-inch cubes
2 cups plain low-fat yogurt
2 tablespoons finely chopped
  cilantro leaves
1 scallion, sliced fine
¼ teaspoon ground dried red
  chilies
½ teaspoon roasted ground cumin
⅛ teaspoon ground black pepper
⅛ teaspoon roasted Basic Garam-
  Masala (see Index)

Add some salt to the cucumber and set in a colander to drain for 15 minutes. Squeeze the excess liquid from the cucumber and place in a bowl. Add the potato, yogurt, cilantro, scallion, ground chili, cumin, pepper, and salt to taste. Mix thoroughly, sprinkle on the garam-masala, and chill. Serve with your choice of entrées.

Yogurt with Spinach

(Palak ka Raita)

2 cups fresh spinach, stems
removed and leaves chopped
fine
2 cups plain low-fat yogurt
1 small onion, peeled and sliced
fine
1 teaspoon roasted ground cumin
¼ teaspoon ground dried red
chilies
⅛ teaspoon ground black pepper
Salt to taste

Steam the spinach over medium heat for 5–7 minutes. In a
bowl, mix together the yogurt, onion, cumin, ground chili,
pepper, and salt. Mix in the spinach and refrigerate. Serve
cold with chicken curry, legumes, and plain rice.

Yogurt Salad

(Raita)

> 2 medium tomatoes, peeled and
>   chopped
> ½ cup peeled and grated cucumber
> 4 radishes, sliced fine
> 4 scallions, sliced fine
> 2 cups plain low-fat yogurt
> ⅛ teaspoon ground dried red
>   chilies
> Salt to taste
> ½ teaspoon paprika

In a bowl, thoroughly mix together all ingredients except paprika. Sprinkle with paprika and refrigerate. Serve chilled with the entrée of your choice.

◇ 6 ◇
Legendary Main-Course Recipes

Hyderabad was truly at one time something from a fairy scene of "Alladin and the Wonderful Lamp." The most famous of the seven nizams (rulers) of Hyderabad was Mahbub Ali Pasha, Nizam Asaf Jah VI, who ascended the throne in 1884 at the age of 17. As time went by, the shy Mahbub Ali Pasha became tired of the constant meddling of British policies and Britain's ceaseless colonial political intrigues, and he withdrew from the affairs of his state. From 1901 until his death in 1911 he left the administration of his state in the hands of his dewan (prime minister), who was an able and trusted friend. The nizam began to spend all of his time in the zenana, where lived the women of the family, more than 300 women employees, and small children.

At the time, Hyderabad was considered the richest state in the world and the nizam the richest man in the world, living a lifestyle of pleasure, glittering extravagance, and luxury only dreamed of in the *Arabian Nights*. It was rumored that the nizam had several hundred concubines whom he supported. His lifestyle is compared to that of an oriental potentate possessing limitless authority. Mahbub Ali Pasha died of alcoholism at the age of 45.

Hyderabad-Style Roast Chicken in Cardamom-Almond-Yogurt Sauce

(Hyderabadi Dahiwala Murgh Elaichi aur Badam)

Serves 6

1 4-pound roasting chicken
1 large onion, peeled and chopped
6 cloves garlic, peeled
¼ cup blanched almonds
1 1-inch piece fresh gingerroot, peeled and chopped
2 dried red chilies, soaked in ¼ cup boiling water for 10 minutes
¼ cup water

1 cup plain low-fat yogurt
¼ cup sour cream
¼ cup vegetable oil
2 cinnamon sticks
10 green cardamom pods
½ teaspoon black peppercorns
10 cloves
5 bay leaves
1 teaspoon paprika
1 teaspoon ground turmeric
Salt to taste

Preheat the oven to 350°F. Remove and discard the skin and fat from the chicken. Place the onion, garlic, almonds, ginger, red chilies, and water in a blender and puree to a fine paste. In a bowl, mix together the yogurt and sour cream.

Heat the oil in a deep saucepan. Add the cinnamon, cardamom, peppercorns, cloves, and bay leaves and fry over medium heat for 5–6 minutes. When the spices turn a shade darker, add the pureed mixture, paprika, turmeric, and salt, stirring and frying for 5 minutes. Add the chicken and brown evenly on all sides for 5–10 minutes. Thoroughly stir in the yogurt-sour cream mixture. Tightly cover and bake for 20 minutes. Turn the chicken over, and bake for another 20 minutes. Remove the lid and let the chicken brown for 5–8 minutes in the oven.

Transfer the chicken to a serving platter and cover with sauce. Serve hot with pilao rice, plain rice, or nan roti and accompanying vegetables and legumes.

Chess, the intellectual game of the world, came from India. Today the outdoor chessboard (where live pieces once moved) in Fatehpur Sikri, the city that Akbar built, which is now a ghost city, remains intact.

When history first recorded the game of chess, it was called *chaturanga*, which literally means "four arms." The old Indian army, prior to the invasion of India by Alexander the Great in 326 B.C., was composed of four arms—chariots, elephants, cavalry, and infantry—each led by a king and his prime minister. The board on which chess was played originally, the ashtapada, was also used for other games played with dice. Chess itself was originally played with dice and was a game of chance. There is also mention of chaturanga being played on a battlefield with opposing teams of live armies: man-driven chariots, live elephants, cavalrymen, and infantrymen. Thus chaturanga was an image of battle, with opposing armies glaring at each other across a neutral no-man's-land.

Emperor's Saffron Chicken
(Padshah Z'affran Murgh)

Serves 4

1 3- to 4-pound roasting chicken
½ teaspoon saffron threads
¼ cup hot milk
1 large onion, peeled and
  chopped
5 cloves garlic, peeled
1 1-inch piece fresh gingerroot,
  peeled and chopped
2 fresh green chilies

¼ cup water
¼ cup vegetable oil
Salt to taste
2 teaspoons roasted
  Mughal-Style
  Garam-Masala (see Index)
1 teaspoon ground cardamom
¼ cup plain low-fat yogurt

Preheat the oven to 350°F. Remove and discard the skin and fat from the chicken.

Soak the saffron threads in the hot milk for 15 minutes. In a blender, puree the onion, garlic, ginger, green chilies, and water to a fine paste. In a medium skillet, heat the oil. Add the pureed mixture and salt and cook over medium heat. When the oil separates from the paste, add the garam-masala and cardamom. Cook for 1 minute, stirring constantly. With a fork, whip the saffron milk into the yogurt and add to the skillet, stirring thoroughly. Cook for 2 minutes and remove the pan from the heat.

Grease a deep aluminum baking pan with oil. Place the chicken in the pan and coat the inside of the chicken with half the sauce mixture; coat the outside with the remaining half. Seal the pan tightly with aluminum foil. Bake for 45 minutes. Remove the foil and bake for another 15 minutes.

Serve hot with pilao rice or plain rice; nan roti, chapatis, parathas, or pooris; and accompanying vegetables and legumes.

Mughal-Style South Indian Spicy Chicken with Onions

(Dakshini Murgh Dopiaza)

Chicken is considered a delicacy in India. This Mughal-style chicken recipe is from my mother's and grandmother's kitchens in Hyderabad and Madras.

Serves 6

12 pieces of chicken (breast, leg, and thigh)
5 large onions, peeled and sliced
6 cloves garlic, peeled
1 1½-inch piece fresh gingerroot, peeled and sliced
3 fresh green chilies
½ cup vegetable oil
3 teaspoons ground cumin
1½ teaspoons ground coriander
1 teaspoon ground turmeric
¼ teaspoon ground dried red chilies
½ teaspoon ground black pepper
Salt to taste
1 teaspoon aniseeds
3 cups chicken stock
½ teaspoon saffron threads
¼ cup hot milk
1 cup plain low-fat yogurt
¼ cup sour cream

Skin the chicken and remove any excess fat.

In a blender, puree half of the sliced onion and all of the garlic, ginger, and green chilies. In a large skillet, heat the oil, add the chicken pieces, and brown evenly on all sides. Remove the chicken and set aside. Heat the oil again and fry the remaining sliced onions over medium heat until they soften. Add the cumin, coriander, turmeric, ground chili, black pepper, salt, and aniseeds. Cook for 3 minutes, stirring frequently. Add the pureed mixture. Cook for another 5 minutes, stirring frequently. Add the chicken pieces and chicken stock. Bring to a boil. Reduce the heat and simmer for 15 minutes.

In the meantime, soak the saffron in the hot milk for 15 minutes. In a bowl, mix together the yogurt and sour cream. Add the saffron milk and yogurt-sour cream mixture to the chicken. Cover and simmer for another 15 minutes or until the chicken is tender and the sauce has thickened.

Serve hot with pilao rice or plain rice; nan roti, chapatis, or pooris; and accompanying vegetables and side dishes.

○

The most famous diamond in the world, the Koh-i-noor (meaning "Mountain of Light"), was found in the Godavari River in South India some 4,000 years ago. It was long reputed to give its owner the crown and rule of the world. At the same time, its possession was supposed to be a hazard to the life of the man who owned it. The curse did not apply if the owner was a woman.

At the time its authentic history began in the 14th century, the Koh-i-noor weighed 186 carats and was clumsily cut. It had been owned for several hundred years by the raja of Malwa (now in Madhya Pradesh). When the Mughals conquered India in 1526, the stone was taken to the treasury at Delhi. It remained there until 1739, when the ruler of Persia, Nadir Shah, invaded India, took Delhi, seized the treasures of the Indian capital, and took the Mughal emperor Muhammad Shah prisoner. A spy-slave informed Nadir Shah that the great Mughal had hidden a diamond of matchless beauty in his turban. Nadir Shah invited his captive to a lavish banquet and, after the meal, suggested that as a gesture of friendship they exchange turbans. Pale, terrified, and ashamed of being discovered, the great Mughal had no choice but to comply. Nadir Shah returned to his quarters, feverishly unwrapped the turban, and found the magnificent Koh-i-noor shining on the cloth.

Nadir Shah returned to Persia with his trophy, but he was assassinated soon afterward. His son and heir was overthrown by a rebellion. Arrested, tortured, and blinded by his enemies, he refused to reveal the hiding place of the Koh-i-noor. When the king of Afghanistan came to his rescue, the dying son of Nadir Shah, soaked in his own blood, handed him the Koh-i-noor.

The king took it back to Afghanistan. Years later his grandson Zaman was deposed, imprisoned, and blinded by his own brother but managed to hide the Koh-i-noor under the floor of his cell. Eventually he escaped with the gem and took refuge at Lahore. There he was received by Ranjit Singh, "Lion of the Punjab," who treated him with great respect but insisted that he give up the Koh-i-noor. Singh had the diamond set in an armlet and wore it. At his death in 1839 it went into the Lahore treasury. It was still there when the Punjab was annexed by the British. In 1849 it was taken by the British East India Company as partial indemnity after the Sikh Wars and was presented to Queen Victoria. At the time, its value was estimated at $700,000. In 1851 Victoria decided to recut the Koh-i-noor. This undertaking required 38 days at a cost of $40,000, and the extraordinary stone was reduced to 108 carats. Today, the Koh-i-noor is still part of the British crown jewels.

Koh-i-Noor Mughal-Style Chicken
(Koh-i-Nur Murgh Musallam)

This recipe could have come from Nadir Shah's kitchen when he entertained his prisoner, Mughal emperor Muhammad Shah, the night they exchanged turbans.

Serves 6

3 pounds chicken thighs and breasts, skinned
3 medium-size fresh green chilies
10 cloves garlic, peeled
1 1-inch piece fresh gingerroot, peeled and chopped
1 teaspoon ground turmeric
1 teaspoon Mughal-Style Garam-Masala (see Index)
Salt to taste
¼ teaspoon ground dried red chilies or cayenne pepper
1 cup plain low-fat yogurt, lightly whipped

12 cloves
12 black peppercorns
2 cinnamon sticks
8 black cardamom pods, pods removed and discarded
16 almonds, shelled
1 teaspoon cumin seeds
2 teaspoons coriander seeds
½ cup vegetable oil
3 large onions, sliced thin
1 cup water
3 large tomatoes, chopped
2 tablespoons chopped cilantro leaves

Remove and discard the fat from the chicken. With a fork, prick the chicken pieces all over. In a blender, grind the green chilies, garlic, and half of the chopped ginger to form a masala paste. Thoroughly rub the chicken with the paste, turmeric, garam-masala, salt, and half of the ground chili. Coat each piece of chicken with yogurt and marinate for 2 hours before cooking.

In a saucepan, roast the cloves, peppercorns, cinnamon, cardamom, almonds, cumin, and coriander (see Index, "Roasting Dry Spices").

Heat the oil in a large pot. Add the onions and fry until golden brown. Remove the onions from the oil and put in a blender or a spice grinder together with all the roasted spices and half of the water. Grind to a fine masala paste.

Heat the same oil that the onions were fried in and brown the chicken pieces, adding the onion-spice paste from the blender. Add the tomatoes and the rest of the ground chili and water. Mix thoroughly. Cover and simmer over medium heat for approximately 30 minutes or until the chicken is tender and the gravy is thick. Garnish with cilantro and serve hot with pilao rice or nan roti and vegetables.

The cuisine of Hyderabad is quite varied and fragrant, consisting of delicious kormas, biryanis, steamed rice and meat, kababs and salans (curries), sour and tangy vegetable preparations, halim (meat and pounded wheat), kulchas (charcoal-oven-baked buns or bread), dals and rasams, almond-flavored desserts (badam ki jali), varieties of halwas, and fragrant betel nut preparations covered with silver paper.

The two kitchens of one of the famous nawabs (rulers) of Hyderabad, Fakhru'l-Mulk II, were housed in a large separate building near his 600-room palace. One kitchen was used for European-style cooking and the other for Indian-style cooking. Goanese cooks prepared European cuisine, while khansamas prepared authentic Mughal and Indian-style dishes. In the Indian-style kitchen a couch was kept for the ladies of the household, who personally gave instructions or supervised the preparation of a biryani or delicate sweetmeat dish. All the cooking was done in silver pots and pans because silver was considered pure.

The following recipe comes from Nawab Fakhru'l-Mulk's kitchen and was served many times in his baradari, a beautiful large room used for family parties and entertainments.

Hyderabad-Style Dried Lamb Curry in Fragrant Spices and Yogurt

(Hyderabadi Korma)

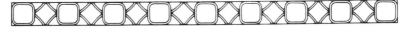

Serves 6

3 pounds boneless lamb or beef, cut into 1-inch cubes
1 large onion, peeled and chopped
1 1-inch piece fresh gingerroot, peeled and chopped
5 cloves garlic, peeled
2 fresh green chilies
¼ cup unsalted raw cashews
¼ cup blanched almonds
½ cup water

2½ teaspoons ground coriander
1½ teaspoons ground cumin
¼ teaspoon ground cinnamon
¼ teaspoon ground cloves
¼ teaspoon ground cardamom
½ teaspoon saffron threads
¼ cup hot milk
¼ cup vegetable oil
Salt to taste
¾ cup plain low-fat yogurt
¼ cup chopped cilantro leaves

Remove and discard the fat from the meat. Place half of the onion, the ginger, garlic, chilies, cashews, almonds, and water in a blender. Puree to a fine paste. Mix in all the ground spices and blend for a few more seconds.

Soak the saffron threads in the hot milk for 15 minutes. Heat the oil in a large saucepan. Add the remaining chopped onions and brown over medium heat, stirring frequently. Add the pureed mixture and fry until the oil begins to separate from the mixture. Stir in the meat, add the salt, and brown evenly on all sides. Mix together the saffron milk and yogurt and stir into the pot with the meat. Reduce the heat and simmer for one hour or until the meat is tender, stirring three or four times to make sure the sauce does not stick to the bottom of the pot.

Garnish with cilantro and serve hot with pilao rice or plain rice; nan roti, parathas, or pooris; and accompanying vegetables and legumes.

◻

Lucknow, the capital of the state of Uttar Pradesh, was a famous center of learning of the nawabs of Oudh (Awadh). Formerly known as the provinces of Oudh and Agra, Oudh was one of the two great states carved out of the decline of the great Mughal Empire by its aristocracy of Persian ancestry. The historic city of Lucknow is quite different from any other city in India because it retains an air of the court of Mughal splendor, royalty, and salutations.

The last nawab of Oudh, Wajid Ali Shah, led a life of opulence, decadence, and scandal. He was extravagant, debauched, and an enormously fat man with several chins. He loved jewelry and wore priceless pear-shaped diamonds, rubies, pearls, and emeralds on his turban, on his fingers, and around his neck. In addition, he spent all of his time in the company of dancing girls, court singers, and young boys and in indulging in rich feasts. In 1856 the British annexed the state of Oudh and took the nawab prisoner for gross mismanagement of his state. For the next 30 years, until his death, the nawab lived in exile in a palace in Calcutta with a huge pension, where he was supplied with all the accoutrements of his taste, but he was deprived of his kingdom.

◻

Lucknow-Style Lamb Patties

(Lucknawi Shami Kabab)

Legend has it that Wajid Ali Shah's favorite dancing girl prepared this shami kabab recipe for her admiring benefactor. Shami kabab can be served as an entrée or hors d'oeuvres.

Serves 5

2 pounds extra-lean ground
  lamb or beef
2 large onions, chopped
1 cup yellow split peas
10 black peppercorns
2 1-inch cinnamon sticks
6 black cardamom pods
8 cloves
4 bay leaves

1 1-inch piece fresh gingerroot,
  peeled and chopped
10 cloves garlic, peeled and
  chopped
3 dried red chilies
3 cups water
1 teaspoon Mughal-Style Garam-
  Masala (see Index)
Salt to taste

Preheat the oven to 350°F. Mix all ingredients together in a large pot and boil over medium heat for about 25 minutes until the meat is tender. Drain and discard the liquid and cool the meat. Remove the cardamom skins and discard.

In a food processor, blend the mixture thoroughly. Make about 20 flat patties.

Lightly grease a flat aluminum pan with vegetable oil and arrange the patties on the pan. Cook for approximately 15 minutes, turn over, and cook the other side 15 minutes, until brown. Serve with Sweet Mint Chutney (see Index), nan roti, rice, and vegetables.

Many of my school friends in Lucknow were children of deposed Muslim nawabs and Hindu maharajas. One friend, Fatima Begum, was the only daughter of a nawab of one of the several smaller principalities of Oudh. Fatima always came to school in a black bur'qa (a tentlike garment worn by Muslim women in public to cover them from head to toe, with eyeholes covered by a fine net) and in purdah (the system of secluding women and veiling them from the sight of men) in a classic old 1920s black Rolls-Royce, the windows of which were covered with black silk curtains. Her chauffeur, who wore a black sherwani (a coat reaching just below his knees that was worn over his pajamas), would always come to fetch us for lunch at the palace or an outing with Fatima.

Fatima's zenana in the huge, airy palace was forbidden to males over 12 years of age except for her father and two brothers. When we were invited for lunch, we were always served in the baradari. Several silver spittoons for betel nut chewing adorned this room. Because Fatima did not entertain many visitors, our presence was always a celebrated treat for her. Spread before us on the dastarkhan (a white calico cloth spread over a Persian carpet for traditional meal service) were 20 different delectable Muslim dishes ranging from koftas to biryanis, four or five varieties of kababs, kormas, three or four varieties of breads, vegetables, legumes, chutneys, and a wild assortment of sweetmeats, followed by an array of scented betel nut preparations. After a four-hour lunch we would retire to Fatima's private quarters to relax on divans, gossip about school, and listen to music as she prepared fresh pan for us from her highly ornamented silver pandan (a metal box containing the ingredients for pan, such as betel leaves, betel nut, fennel seeds, cardamom, cloves, cinnamon, lime, and perfumed coconut flakes).

Oudh-Style Curried Meatballs
(Awadhi Kofta Kari)

Serves 6

8 cloves garlic, peeled
1 1-inch piece fresh gingerroot, peeled and chopped
2 fresh green chilies
3 teaspoons poppy seeds
2 teaspoons roasted Mughal-Style Garam-Masala (see Index)
¼ teaspoon ground black pepper
Salt to taste
1 teaspoon paprika
½ cup water
3 pounds lean ground lamb or beef
2 eggs, beaten lightly

¼ cup chick-pea flour
¼ cup vegetable oil
1 large onion, peeled and chopped
1 teaspoon ground turmeric
¼ teaspoon ground dried red chilies
1 teaspoon ground cumin
2 teaspoons ground coriander
3 medium tomatoes, peeled and chopped
½ cup plain low-fat yogurt
¼ cup chopped cilantro leaves

Place the garlic, ginger, green chilies, poppy seeds, garam-masala, ground pepper, salt, paprika, and water in a blender. Puree to a fine paste. In a large bowl, thoroughly mix the meat, pureed mixture, eggs, and chick-pea flour. Form 20 medium-sized meatballs and set aside.

Heat the oil in a deep skillet. Add the onion and fry over medium heat until browned. Add the turmeric, ground chili, cumin, and coriander and stir. Add the tomatoes and cook until soft. Gently add the meatballs and bring the mixture to a boil. Add the yogurt, reduce the heat to medium-low, and cook for 20 minutes. Turn the meatballs over and cook for another 20 minutes.

Garnish with the cilantro and serve hot with pilao rice or plain rice; nan roti, parathas, or pooris; and accompanying vegetables and legumes.

Legend has it that Jahangir, "Conqueror of the World"
(1605–1627), told his empress, Nur Jahan, that she could
rule his empire if she allowed him wine and meat.

His nearly-23-year rule was more or less an undisturbed
life of indolent luxury, and he built the famous Peacock
Throne that was completed by his son, Shah Jahan, whose
fascination for jewels preceded his fascination for the
women of his harem.

The French jeweler Jean-Baptiste Tavernier, who bought
and sold gems from the Mughal courts, described the Peacock Throne in 1665. According to him, the throne was six
feet long and four feet wide and blazed with diamonds and
rubies. Four bars of gold were attached to the top of the legs
and supported the base of the throne. There were 12 gold
columns that also supported a canopy. Three sides were
closed, and one side was left open to face the court. The
entire throne was covered with inlaid gold and set with
priceless diamonds and large rubies and emeralds. The emperor sat cross-legged in the middle with a flat cushion
(takiya) on either side of him. One of the Mughal's weapons
was attached to each column of the throne: his sword, a
quiver with arrows, a mace, and a round shield. The pillows,
as well as the weapons and steps, were covered with gems to
match the throne. Over the emperor's seat was a canopy
smothered with diamonds and pearls, and above that stood
the gem-studded body of a gold peacock.

The magnificent Peacock Throne was taken by Nadir
Shah to Persia in 1739 when he pillaged Delhi and left it in
ruins. Before Nadir Shah was murdered, he had the throne
duplicated and broke the original Peacock Throne into
pieces.

Emperor Jahangir's Lamb Curry

(Shahi Padshah Korma)

Serves 6

3 pounds boneless lamb, cut into 1-inch cubes
3¼ cups water
2 2-inch cinnamon sticks
3 bay leaves
1 teaspoon black peppercorns
Salt to taste
2 tablespoons fresh lemon juice
6 cloves garlic, peeled
1 2-inch piece fresh gingerroot, peeled and chopped
15 green cardamom pods, pods removed and discarded
8 cloves
1¼ tablespoons coriander seeds
¼ cup vegetable oil
1 large onion, sliced thin
1 cup plain low-fat yogurt
¼ cup sour cream
½ teaspoon saffron threads
¼ cup blanched almonds
¼ cup raisins

Remove and discard the fat from the meat. In a large pot, place the lamb, 3 cups of the water, the cinnamon sticks, bay leaves, peppercorns, salt, and lemon juice. Boil for 20 minutes. Reserve the lamb and stock separately. In a blender, puree the garlic, ginger, cardamom seeds, cloves, coriander seeds, and remaining ¼ cup water.

Heat the oil in a large saucepan. Add the onion and fry over medium heat until soft. Add the pureed mixture and stir for 5 minutes. Add the boiled lamb and stir for another 5 minutes. Add the meat stock. Mix together the yogurt and sour cream and add to the lamb. Mix thoroughly, cover, and cook for 30 minutes. Remove the lid and stir in the saffron threads, almonds, and raisins. Cook for another 10 minutes or until the lamb is tender.

Serve hot with pilao rice or plain rice; nan roti, pooris, parathas, or chapatis; and vegetables.

◯

    Among the many fascinating legends told about the origin of chess is the story of Sissa, a scientist and the inventor of the game. In western India, Raja Balhait had asked his advisers to create a game that demonstrated the values of prudence, diligence, foresight, and knowledge. Sissa brought a chessboard to the raja and explained that he had chosen war as a model for the game because war was the most effective school in which to learn the values of decision, vigor, endurance, circumspection, and courage. The raja was delighted with the game and ordered its preservation in temples. He considered its principles the foundation of all justice and held it to be the best training in the art of war.

    The raja said to his subject Sissa, "Ask any reward. It will be yours." Being a scientist, Sissa felt rewarded by the pleasure his invention was giving others; but the king insisted, and finally Sissa said, "Give me a reward in grains of corn on the chessboard [ashtapada]. On the first square one grain, on the second two, on the third four, on the fourth double of that, and so on until the 64th and last square."

    The raja would not hear of it. He insisted that Sissa ask for something of more worth than grains of corn. But Sissa insisted he had no need of much and that the grains of corn would suffice. Thereupon the raja ordered the corn to be brought; but before they had reached the 30th square, all the corn of India was exhausted. Perturbed, he looked at Sissa, who laughed and told his raja that he knew perfectly well he could never receive the reward he had asked because the amount of corn involved would cover the whole surface of the earth to a depth of nine inches.

    The raja did not know which to admire more: the invention of chess or the ingenuity of Sissa's request. The number involved is 18,446,744,073,709,551,615 grains. This number had been previously calculated by the early Indian mathematicians, who, incidentally, had invented the decimal system long before it reached the Arabs and the West.

◯

Spicy Mughal-Style Lamb in Almond Sauce

(Mughalai Kheema Masala)

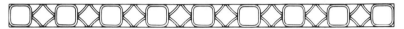

Serves 6

¼ cup vegetable oil
1 large onion, peeled and chopped fine
6 cloves garlic, peeled and chopped fine
1 1-inch piece fresh gingerroot, peeled and chopped fine
2 fresh green chilies, chopped fine
8 cloves
10 green cardamom pods
4 bay leaves
2 cinnamon sticks
1 teaspoon poppy seeds
½ teaspoon black peppercorns

2½ teaspoons Mughal-Style Garam-Masala (see Index)
2 teaspoons ground cumin
4 teaspoons ground coriander
1½ teaspoons ground turmeric
1 teaspoon paprika
¼ cup blanched almonds, ground to a paste
1 large tomato, peeled and chopped
3 pounds lean ground lamb
1 cup plain low-fat yogurt
Salt to taste
¼ cup finely chopped fresh mint leaves

Heat the oil in a large skillet. Add the onion, garlic, ginger, and green chilies and fry over medium heat until the onion has browned. Add the cloves, cardamom, bay leaves, cinnamon, poppy seeds, and peppercorns. Stirring constantly, cook for about 2 minutes, until the spices become a shade darker. Add the garam-masala, cumin, coriander, turmeric, and paprika and stir for 2 minutes longer. Add the almond paste and tomato. Mix the ingredients thoroughly. Add the meat, yogurt, and salt, stirring with a spatula. Cover and cook for 20 minutes, stirring occasionally.

Garnish with fresh mint leaves and serve hot with plain basmati rice or nan roti and accompanying vegetables and legumes.

Mughal-Style Fragrant Saffron Rice Layered with Spicy Lamb

(Mughalai Biryani Gosht)

A biryani is a rice and lamb dish blended with aromatic spices. Biryanis require at least three to four hours to prepare and are often accompanied by vegetables and nan or chapatis. Traditionally biryani is prepared during festivals, weddings, and banquets or when entertaining favorite guests.

This particular recipe for biryani is from the royal kitchens of Akbar the Great at Fatehpur Sikri (1571). Akbar often ate at irregular times of the day, giving his kitchens hardly any warning of when he desired to dine. The kitchens therefore operated around the clock.

Serves 10

Lamb

5 pounds boneless leg of lamb, cut into 1-inch cubes
2 teaspoons ground turmeric
¼ cup vegetable oil
4 large onions, sliced
10 cloves garlic, peeled and chopped
1 2-inch piece fresh gingerroot, peeled and chopped fine
¼ cup Basic Curry Powder (see Index)
½ teaspoon ground dried red chilies
2 tablespoons fresh lemon juice
Salt to taste
1½ teaspoons Mughal-Style Garam-Masala (see Index)
1¼ teaspoons ground cardamom
3 fresh green chilies
½ cup chopped fresh mint leaves
5 tomatoes, peeled and chopped
¼ cup chopped cilantro leaves

Rice Pilao

¼ cup vegetable oil
2 medium onions, sliced
2 2-inch cinnamon sticks
10 green cardamom pods
10 cloves
8 bay leaves
2 teaspoons cumin seeds

1½ quarts meat broth or water
4 cups long-grain basmati rice,
    rinsed and soaked in cold water
    for 2 hours
⅛ teaspoon ground nutmeg
½ teaspoon saffron threads
¼ cup blanched almonds

Prepare the lamb: Coat the meat with the turmeric and let stand for 15 minutes at room temperature. Heat the oil in a large saucepan. Add the onions, garlic, and ginger and fry over medium heat until the onions are soft and golden brown. Add the curry powder and the ground dried red chilies and fry for a minute or 2 longer; then stir in the lemon juice and salt. Add the meat, stirring it until it is coated with the onion mixture. Add the garam-masala, cardamom, green chilies, mint, and tomatoes. Cover and simmer over low heat for an hour, stirring occasionally. When the lamb is tender and as thick as a curry, turn off the heat. Garnish with cilantro leaves and let stand while you prepare the rice.

Prepare the rice pilao: Preheat the oven to 250°F.

Heat the oil in a large pot. Add the onions, cinnamon, cardamom, cloves, and bay leaves and fry over medium heat until golden brown. Add the cumin seeds and continue frying until the onions are dark brown. Add the broth or water and bring to a boil. Add the rice, nutmeg, and saffron and cook, covered, over medium heat until all the liquid is absorbed and the rice is cooked. Remove half of the rice from the pot and place it on a large plate. Place the lamb biryani on the rice in the pot and cover it with the remaining rice. Cover the mixture with a damp cheesecloth or aluminum foil to seal in the steam and place a lid on the pot. Bake for 10 minutes. Serve hot, garnished with blanched almonds.

Before India's independence in 1947 Hyderabad was
the largest and wealthiest Indian state, and the Paigah
nobles, or the great Nobles of the Realm, lived in opulence
and glittering splendor on a scale that exceeded that of any
European monarch in any era.

A day in the life of a famous Great Noble of the Realm
began as follows: The nawab, who had a mighty appetite,
would awaken at 4:00 in the morning. After spending an
hour exercising, he would consume two quarts of fresh
buffalo milk along with two pills of opium, a practice
shared by many in the nizam's court. (At the time, many
people over 40–45 years of age took opium to soothe aches
and pains, rheumatism, old wounds, gout, or other age-
related infirmities.)

A few minutes after eating the pills, the nawab would
ride for an hour. By 7:00 he returned, bathed, and dressed
for the day. In the mardana (men's quarters) he was served
a European-style breakfast of liver, kidneys, or fish, toast,
marmalade, jam, and tea or coffee. The nawab also ate six
poached eggs. When breakfast wore off at around 11:00, the
nawab was given his almond paste, which consisted of 75
almonds and sugar made into a paste and piled on a large
spoon. After performing the ceremonial salams and attend-
ing to his various state duties, he returned at 1:00 for lunch,
which was served in the zenana (women's quarters or
harem). His lunch consisted of two European-style soups
and seven or eight Indian-style dishes such as biryani,
korma, kababs, legumes, vegetables, seafood curries, chutneys, and yogurt salads. That was followed by an Indian
dessert, a European dessert, and fresh fruits. The nawab
rested in the mardana, and the newspaper was read to him
by a courtier (musahib). At 3:30 he had a cup of tea and
went on state visits. Upon his return at 6:00 in the evening,
his almond paste would be waiting for him. For two hours
he received callers, and after changing into Indian-style
clothes he would be ready to eat dinner with his family.

Hyderabad-Style Saffron Rice Layered with Fragrant Lamb

(Hyderabadi Biryani Gosht)

It was said that if any Paigah noble wished to leave Hyderabad, his petitions to the nizam were frequently dismissed, rejected, or mysteriously lost. As a result, in frustration many turned to domestic pursuits such as conspiracies, concubines, gambling, and even cookery. This famous recipe is from one such Paigah noble khansama.

Serves 6

2 pounds boneless lean lamb, cut into 1-inch cubes
2 pounds long-grain basmati rice
6 cloves garlic, peeled
1 1-inch piece fresh gingerroot, peeled and chopped
2 fresh green chilies
¼ cup chopped cilantro leaves
¼ cup chopped fresh mint leaves
10 cloves
2 cinnamon sticks
1 teaspoon cumin seeds
½ teaspoon ground nutmeg

10 green cardamom pods, pods removed and discarded
1 teaspoon saffron threads
¼ cup hot milk
½ cup vegetable oil
3 large onions, peeled and sliced fine
½ teaspoon ground dried red chilies
Juice of 1 lemon
2 cups plain low-fat yogurt
Salt to taste
2½ quarts water

Remove and discard the fat from the meat. Rinse the rice 8–10 times in cold water and soak in water for 30 minutes. Drain and set aside. In a blender, puree the garlic, ginger, green chilies, cilantro, and mint leaves. In a spice or coffee grinder, grind 5 of the cloves, 1 of the cinnamon sticks, the cumin seeds, nutmeg, and seeds from 4 of the cardamom pods. Soak the saffron threads in the hot milk for 15 minutes.

Heat the oil in a large saucepan. Add the onions and brown over medium heat. Remove the onions and drain on paper towels, reserving the oil in the pan. In a large bowl, mix the pureed mixture with the meat. Add the ground chili, lemon juice, yogurt, salt, powdered spices, and half of the browned onions. Mix thoroughly and marinate in the refrigerator for 4 hours.

Heat the oil again and add the meat and marinade. Bring to a boil. Reduce the heat, cover, and cook for 1 hour, stirring occasionally, until the meat is tender and the gravy is thick. While the meat is cooking, in another pot heat the water and add the remaining cardamom, cloves, and cinnamon stick and salt to taste. When the water is boiling, add the rice and cook for 5 to 7 minutes. Remove and drain in a colander.

Preheat the oven to 350°F. Lightly grease the bottom and sides of a large casserole dish. Spread an even layer of rice over the bottom and then spread the cooked meat and gravy over the first layer of rice. Cover the meat and gravy with another layer of rice. With a spoon, pour the saffron milk over the rice and garnish with the remaining browned onions. Cover with aluminum foil and the casserole lid and bake for 30–40 minutes, until the rice is done. Serve hot, with or without side dishes.

◇ 7 ◇
Meat and Poultry Curries

Muslim-Style Fragrant and Spicy Beef Meatballs

(Hussainee Kofta Kari)

Serves 6

3 pounds lean ground beef
6 cloves garlic, peeled and
  crushed
Salt to taste
1 teaspoon paprika
¼ cup vegetable oil
6 cloves
6 green cardamom pods
8 black peppercorns
2 cinnamon sticks
4 bay leaves

¼ teaspoon ground nutmeg
2 teaspoons Mughal-Style Garam-
  Masala (see Index)
1 large onion, peeled and
  chopped fine
3 medium tomatoes, quartered
½ teaspoon ground dried red
  chilies
¼ cup plain low-fat yogurt
2 cups water
¼ cup chopped cilantro leaves

In a large bowl, thoroughly mix the ground meat, garlic, salt, and paprika. Form the mixture into 24 uniformly sized balls. Heat the oil in a large saucepan. Add the cloves, cardamom, peppercorns, cinnamon, bay leaves, nutmeg, and garam-masala and fry over medium heat for 3 minutes. Add the onion and cook until golden brown. Stir in the tomatoes and ground chili and cook for 2 minutes. Add the yogurt and mix thoroughly. Add the water and bring to a boil. Gently drop in the meatballs and, with a spoon, cover the meatballs with sauce. Cover and simmer for 20 minutes. Remove the lid and cook the meatballs for another 5 minutes. Garnish with cilantro leaves and serve hot.

Shafi's Famous Lamb Curry
(Shafi ka Shali Gosht)

Serves 6

3 pounds boneless lamb shoulder, cut into 1-inch cubes
1 tablespoon coriander seeds
1 teaspoon cumin seeds
1 tablespoon poppy seeds
¼ cup blanched almonds
¼ teaspoon black peppercorns
4 black cardamom pods, pods removed and discarded
5 cloves
¼ teaspoon ground mace
¼ cup freshly grated coconut
3 dried red chilies, soaked in ¼ cup hot water for 15 minutes

1 1-inch piece fresh gingerroot, peeled and chopped
8 cloves garlic, peeled
2 cups water
¼ cup vegetable oil
4 bay leaves
2 cinnamon sticks
6 green cardamom pods, pods removed and discarded
1 large onion, peeled and grated
1 teaspoon ground turmeric
¾ cup plain low-fat yogurt
3 medium tomatoes, peeled and chopped

Remove and discard the fat from the meat. Place the coriander, cumin, poppy seeds, almonds, peppercorns, black cardamom seeds, cloves, mace, and coconut in a pan and roast over medium heat. Remove and puree in a blender with the red chilies in their soaking water and the ginger, garlic, and ¼ cup of the water.

Heat the oil in a large saucepan. Add the bay leaves, cinnamon, and crushed green cardamom seeds and fry over medium heat for 1 minute. Add the grated onion and fry until brown. Mix in the pureed mixture and turmeric. Cook for 5 minutes. Slowly add the yogurt, stirring thoroughly for 5 minutes. Stir in the meat and the tomatoes, mix, and add the remaining water. Reduce the heat, cover, and cook for 40 minutes or until the meat is tender.

Serve hot with pilao rice or plain rice, nan roti, vegetables, and raita.

Goan Portuguese-Style Spicy Pork
(Shikar Vindaloo)

*This dish was originally concocted by the Portuguese settlers
in India. Today the Goanese have perfected this dish to
something quite out of this world. One of the tastiest curries
ever invented, it is slightly spicier than the average curry but
utterly delectable.*

Serves 6

3 pounds boneless lean pork, cut
into 1-inch cubes

3 teaspoons roasted ground
cumin

2 teaspoons roasted ground black
mustard seeds

1 teaspoon roasted ground
turmeric

½ teaspoon roasted ground black
pepper

¾ teaspoon roasted ground
cinnamon

¾ teaspoon roasted ground
cardamom

½ teaspoon roasted ground cloves

½ teaspoon roasted ground
nutmeg

1 large onion, peeled and
chopped

10 cloves garlic, peeled

1 1-inch piece fresh gingerroot,
peeled and chopped

1 teaspoon paprika

6 dried red chilies, soaked in 2
tablespoons of the cider
vinegar for 15 minutes

¼ cup mustard oil or vegetable
oil

1 cup cider vinegar

1 tablespoon light brown sugar
(optional)

Salt to taste

Remove and discard the fat from the meat. Put the roasted
spices in a blender with the onion, garlic, ginger, paprika,
red chilies with the vinegar they soaked in, 2 tablespoons of
the oil, the rest of the vinegar, the brown sugar, and salt and
puree. In a large bowl, mix the pureed mixture with the
pork and marinate overnight in the refrigerator.

Heat the remaining oil in a large saucepan. Add the meat cubes and fry over medium heat until the meat is browned evenly. Pour in the marinade mixture and stir for 5 minutes, until the oil separates from the masala. Reduce the heat, cover, and simmer for 45–60 minutes, until the meat is tender. Serve with plain rice and accompanying vegetables and pappadams.

Lamb with Spinach in Yogurt Sauce
(Dahiwala Sag Gosht)

If desired, beef stew meat may be substituted for lamb.

Serves 6

3 pounds boneless lean lamb stew meat, cut into 1-inch cubes
¼ cup vegetable oil
1½ tablespoons black mustard seeds
1 tablespoon green cardamom seeds
1 tablespoon ground coriander
½ teaspoon crushed black peppercorns
2 fresh green chilies, chopped

6 cloves garlic, peeled and crushed
1 1-inch piece fresh gingerroot, peeled and chopped
1 large onion, peeled and chopped
1 teaspoon ground turmeric
3 pounds fresh spinach, washed and chopped
Salt to taste
¼ cup plain low-fat yogurt

Remove and discard the fat from the meat. Preheat the oven to 350°F. Heat the oil in a large saucepan over medium heat and add the mustard seeds. When they start popping, add the cardamom, coriander, pepper, chilies, garlic, and ginger. Fry for about 1 minute. Stir in the meat and brown evenly for about 10 minutes. Add the onion and fry until browned. Stir in the turmeric, spinach, and salt. Stir the yogurt thoroughly into the meat and spinach. Cook for 5 minutes.

Transfer the meat and spinach to a large casserole and cover. Bake for 30 minutes, until the lamb is tender. Serve hot with pilao rice or plain rice, chapatis or nan roti, and accompanying legumes and pappadams.

Spiced Liver
(Masaledar Kaleja)

Serves 6

3 pounds calf's or lamb's liver
1 tablespoon all-purpose
  unbleached flour
Juice of 1 small lemon
½ teaspoon crushed black
  peppercorns
¼ cup vegetable oil
2 large onions, peeled and grated
8 cloves garlic, peeled and grated
1 1-inch piece fresh gingerroot,
  peeled and grated
1 teaspoon ground turmeric
2 tablespoons cider vinegar
½ teaspoon ground dried red
  chilies
Salt to taste

Cut the liver into 2-inch-long strips. Sprinkle the flour on a flat pan and lay the strips of liver on top. Squeeze the juice of the lemon over the liver and sprinkle with crushed peppercorns. Heat the oil in a large saucepan. Add the onions, garlic, and ginger and fry over medium heat until the onions are browned. Stir in the turmeric, vinegar, and ground chili. Add the liver and salt and mix gently with a spatula. Reduce the heat, cover, and simmer for 20 minutes. (The secret to cooking liver is to cook it as slowly as possible to prevent it from becoming tough.) Serve hot with plain rice, pappadams, and accompanying vegetables and legumes.

Spicy Kerala Chicken Curry

(Kerala Kozhi Kuttan)

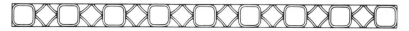

Serves 6

1 4-pound chicken
2 teaspoons ground turmeric
Salt to taste
¼ cup plain low-fat yogurt
2 cups freshly grated coconut
1 cup coconut liquid
¼ cup vegetable oil
10 cloves garlic, peeled
1 1-inch piece fresh gingerroot, peeled and chopped
½ teaspoon black peppercorns
1 teaspoon aniseeds

2 cinnamon sticks
10 cloves
5 teaspoons coriander seeds
2 teaspoons cumin seeds
1 large onion, peeled and chopped
6 dried red chilies, soaked in ½ cup hot water for 15 minutes
2 medium tomatoes, peeled and pureed
3 cups water

Remove the skin and fat from the chicken. Cut it into 10–12 pieces and place in a large bowl. Rub the turmeric, salt, and yogurt into the chicken and set aside. Soak the grated coconut in the coconut liquid and set aside. Heat 1 tablespoon of the oil in a medium saucepan. Add the garlic, ginger, peppercorns, aniseeds, cinnamon, cloves, coriander, and cumin and roast. Place the roasted spices in a blender, add ¼ cup of the coconut mixture, and puree.

Heat the remaining oil in a large pot. Add the onion and fry over medium heat until browned. Add the pureed mixture, chilies (drained), and tomato puree and cook, stirring thoroughly, for about 5 minutes. Mix in the chicken pieces and stir for another 5 minutes. Add the rest of the coconut mixture, cover, and bring to a boil. Uncover and slowly mix in the water. Reduce the heat, cover, and cook for 25 minutes, until the chicken is tender. Serve hot with plain rice and accompanying vegetables.

Chicken Curry in Yogurt Mint Sauce
(Dahi Pudina Murgh)

Serves 6

1 4-pound chicken	8 cloves
1 teaspoon ground turmeric	4 bay leaves
Salt to taste	2 cinnamon sticks
½ cup plain low-fat yogurt	½ teaspoon black peppercorns
¼ cup vegetable oil	3 teaspoons Basic Garam-Masala
1 large onion, peeled and grated	(see Index)
6 cloves garlic, peeled and grated	1 teaspoon paprika
1 1-inch piece fresh gingerroot,	¼ teaspoon ground nutmeg
peeled and grated	2 cups chicken stock
8 green cardamom pods	¼ cup chopped fresh mint leaves

Remove the skin and fat from the chicken and cut into 10–
12 pieces. Boil the neck, wings, and giblets to make stock.
Place the chicken in a large bowl. Rub the turmeric, salt,
and yogurt over the chicken and set aside to marinate for 1
hour.

Heat the oil in a large pot. Add the onion, garlic, and ginger
and fry over medium heat until the onion is browned. Add
the cardamom, cloves, bay leaves, cinnamon, and peppercorns and stir for 2 minutes. Add the garam-masala, paprika, and nutmeg and mix thoroughly for 3 minutes. Add
the chicken and yogurt marinade and the chicken stock and
stir. Cover and simmer for 45 minutes, until the chicken is
tender. Add the mint leaves, cover, and cook for 5 minutes.
Serve hot with pilao rice or plain rice; nan roti, chapatis,
parathas, or pooris; accompanying vegetables, and legumes.

Chicken Curry in Cashew Sauce
(Murgh Kaju Masala)

Serves 6

1 4-pound chicken
¼ cup vegetable oil
2 large onions, peeled and grated
8 cloves garlic, peeled and grated
1 1-inch piece fresh gingerroot,
  peeled and grated
2 fresh green chilies, grated
3 tablespoons Basic Curry Powder
  (see Index)
2 teaspoons Basic Garam-Masala
  (see Index)

Salt to taste
1 teaspoon ground turmeric
1 teaspoon paprika
¼ cup raw cashews, ground to a
  fine paste
2 cups chicken stock
¼ cup plain low-fat yogurt
4 medium tomatoes, peeled and
  chopped
¼ cup cilantro leaves (optional)

Remove the skin and fat from the chicken and cut into 10–12 pieces. In a small pot, boil the chicken neck, giblets, and wings to make stock.

Heat the oil in a large saucepan. Add the onions, garlic, ginger, and chilies and fry over medium heat until the onions are browned. Add the curry powder, garam-masala, salt, turmeric, paprika, and cashew paste and stir thoroughly. Cook for 5 minutes, until the oil separates from the masala. Add the stock, mix, and cook for 3 minutes. Mix in the yogurt, tomatoes, and chicken and stir thoroughly. Cover and simmer for 40 minutes, until the chicken is tender, occasionally stirring and checking to be sure the sauce does not stick to the bottom of the pan.

Garnish with cilantro leaves and serve hot with pilao rice or plain rice; nan roti, chapatis, pooris, or parathas; and accompanying vegetables and legumes.

Madras-Style Chicken Curry
(Madrasi Murgh Korma)

Serves 6

1 4-pound chicken
1 teaspoon ground turmeric
Salt to taste
¼ cup plain low-fat yogurt
1 cup water
2 large onions, peeled and chopped
10 cloves garlic, peeled
1 1-inch piece fresh gingerroot, peeled and chopped
2 dried red chilies
4 teaspoons coriander seeds
2 teaspoons cumin seeds

½ cup freshly grated coconut
6 cloves
½ teaspoon black peppercorns
6 black cardamom pods, pods removed and discarded
1 cinnamon stick, broken into small pieces
¼ teaspoon ground nutmeg
½ teaspoon black mustard seeds
½ teaspoon fenugreek seeds
2 bay leaves
¼ cup vegetable oil
¼ cup cilantro leaves

Remove the skin and fat from the chicken. Cut into 10–12 pieces and place in a large bowl. Rub the turmeric, salt, and yogurt over the chicken and marinate for 1 hour.

Place the water, onions, garlic, ginger, red chilies, coriander, cumin, coconut, cloves, peppercorns, cardamom, cinnamon, nutmeg, mustard seeds, fenugreek seeds, and bay leaves in a blender and puree. Heat the oil in a large saucepan, add the pureed mixture, and fry over medium heat for 10 minutes. When the oil separates from the masala, stir in the chicken and yogurt marinade and mix thoroughly. Bring to a boil, reduce the heat, cover, and simmer for 45 minutes, until the chicken is tender, occasionally stirring and checking to be sure the sauce does not stick to the bottom of the pan. Garnish with cilantro and serve hot with plain rice,

Spicy Chicken Roast
(Murgh Masala)

Serves 6

1 4-pound chicken
Salt to taste
1 teaspoon paprika
½ cup water
1 large onion, peeled and
   chopped
6 cloves garlic, peeled
1 1-inch piece fresh gingerroot,
   peeled and chopped
1 teaspoon ground turmeric
2 tablespoons Basic Garam-
   Masala (see Index)
1 tablespoon ground coriander
2 teaspoons ground cumin
½ teaspoon ground dried red
   chilies
¼ cup vegetable oil
2 cups chicken stock
¼ cup sour cream
½ cup plain low-fat yogurt

Remove the skin and fat from the chicken. Rub salt and
paprika inside and over the chicken and set aside. Boil the
wings, neck, and giblets to make stock. Place the water,
onion, garlic, ginger, turmeric, garam-masala, coriander,
cumin, and ground chili in a blender and puree.

Preheat the oven to 400°F. Heat the oil in a medium saucepan. Add the pureed mixture and fry for about 10 minutes, until the oil separates. Add the stock and cook for another 5 minutes. In a small bowl, mix the sour cream and yogurt and stir it into the stock mixture. Bring to a boil and remove from the heat. Grease a deep roasting pan, place the chicken in the center, and rub the yogurt mixture over and inside the cavity of the chicken. Cover tightly with aluminum foil and bake for 20 minutes. Reduce the heat to 350°F, baste the chicken, and bake for another 15 minutes. Remove the foil, baste the chicken, and bake it, uncovered, for another 10 minutes to brown it.

Serve hot with pilao or plain rice; nan roti, chapatis, pooris, or parathas; and accompanying vegetables and legumes.

Roast Chicken Marinated in Yogurt and Lemon Masala

(Tandoori Murgh)

You can substitute Cornish game hens for the chicken in this recipe.

Serves 6

2 3-pound roasting chickens
Salt to taste
2 teaspoons paprika
Juice of 3 lemons
1 teaspoon saffron threads
2 tablespoons hot water
4 teaspoons coriander seeds
2 teaspoons cumin seeds
1 teaspoon ground turmeric
¼ teaspoon ground dried red
  chilies
2 tablespoons Basic Garam-
  Masala (see Index)
2 cups plain low-fat yogurt
2 tablespoons vegetable oil
6 cloves garlic, peeled
1 1-inch piece fresh gingerroot,
  peeled and chopped
1 fresh green chili

Remove the skin and fat from the chickens. With a sharp knife, make ½-inch slits all over the chickens. Place the chickens in a large bowl, and rub with salt and paprika. Squeeze the juice of the lemons inside and over the chickens. Allow to marinate for 30 minutes. Soak the saffron threads in the hot water for 15 minutes.

In a small saucepan, roast the coriander, cumin, turmeric, ground chili, and garam-masala. Place the yogurt, oil, garlic, ginger, green chili, and roasted spices in a blender and puree. Add the saffron water and blend for 30 seconds. Spread this masala over and inside the chickens, cover with aluminum foil, and marinate overnight in the refrigerator.

Preheat the oven to 400°F. Grease a deep aluminum pan and place the chickens in the center. Pour the marinade over the chickens. Roast, uncovered, for 15 minutes, reduce the heat to 350°F, baste the chickens, and roast for 30 minutes, until the chickens are dark red. Remove the chickens and carve into pieces. If the chickens are still pink inside, place back in the oven and cook for another 10 minutes.

Serve immediately with nan roti, the chutney of your choice, salat (slices of onion, cucumber, radish, tomato, and green chilies sprinkled with lemon juice), and accompanying vegetables and legumes if desired.

To barbecue the chicken: Marinate six chicken legs and six breasts in the tandoori sauce. Light the barbecue grill, using a 2-inch-thick layer of charcoal. When the coals are red-hot, place the chicken on the grill and cook for 10 minutes. Remove and dip in the marinade mixture. Barbecue on the other side for 10 minutes. Serve hot with nan roti, which you can also heat on the grill.

Roast Duck with Pistachios
(Masala Pista Vath)

Serves 6

1 6-pound duck
Juice of 1 lemon
¼ cup sour cream
8 cloves garlic, peeled and
   crushed
1 teaspoon ground turmeric
1 teaspoon paprika
Salt to taste
½ teaspoon ground dried red
   chilies
½ teaspoon saffron threads
¼ cup hot milk
2 large potatoes, peeled, boiled,
   and mashed
¼ cup vegetable oil
2 large onions, chopped fine
1 1-inch piece fresh gingerroot,
   peeled and chopped fine

2 fresh green chilies, chopped
   fine
¼ cup finely chopped unsalted
   pistachios
½ cup finely chopped fresh mint
   leaves
1 tablespoon ground coriander
2 teaspoons ground cumin
1 tablespoon Basic Garam-Masala
   (see Index)
½ teaspoon ground nutmeg
1 teaspoon ground black mustard
   seeds
½ teaspoon crushed black
   peppercorns

Cut the wings off the duck. Cut the giblets into small pieces
and boil the neck, wings, and giblets in a small pot of water
until the meat is tender and separates from the bones. Remove the meat and set the meat and stock aside to cool. In a
bowl, mix the lemon juice with the sour cream, garlic,
turmeric, paprika, salt, and ground chili. Rub this mixture
all over the duck and inside the cavity and marinate for 2
hours at room temperature.

Preheat the oven to 400°F.

Soak the saffron threads in the hot milk for 15 minutes.

Remove the skin and bones from the giblet stock and mix the stock with the mashed potatoes. Heat the oil in a saucepan. Add the onions, ginger, green chilies, pistachios, and mint leaves and cook over medium heat until the onions are browned. Stir in the coriander, cumin, garam-masala, nutmeg, mustard seeds, and crushed pepper and fry for about 5 minutes, stirring constantly. Add the cooked giblets and mashed potatoes and stir for 5 minutes. Turn off the heat.

Place the duck in a large deep casserole or roasting pan. Stuff the cavity of the duck with the mashed potato and giblet masala and secure with skewers. Pour the saffron milk over the duck and cover the pan with foil and the lid. Bake for 30 minutes. Reduce the heat to 300°F and bake for another 30 minutes. Remove the lid and foil and baste the duck. Cover and bake for another hour, until the duck is tender. Remove the lid and foil and brown evenly in the oven for 30 minutes, turning the duck over after 15 minutes.

Serve hot with plain rice, nan roti, and accompanying vegetables.

◇ 8 ◇

Seafood Curries

Mughal-Style Fish Curry in Almond Sauce

(Mughalai Pomfret)

Using your culinary discretion, you may replace whole fish with shrimps, salmon steak, lobster, or crab.

Serves 6

2 large fresh pomfrets or fish of
  your choice
1 1-inch piece fresh gingerroot,
  peeled and chopped
6 cloves garlic, peeled
Salt to taste
1 tablespoon black mustard seeds
Juice of 1 lemon
¼ cup vegetable oil
1 large onion, peeled and
  chopped
¼ cup hot water
¼ cup blanched almonds
2 tablespoons coriander seeds
2 teaspoons cumin seeds
2 dried red chilies
1 teaspoon ground turmeric
½ teaspoon saffron threads
¼ cup hot milk
6 green cardamom pods
1 cinnamon stick
½ teaspoon black peppercorns
2 bay leaves
¼ teaspoon whole cloves
¼ cup plain low-fat yogurt

Make incisions 1 inch apart on both sides of the fish from head to tail. Place the ginger, garlic, salt, mustard seeds, and lemon juice in a blender and puree. Set the fish on a flat dish and spread the pureed mixture over and into the fish. Marinate in the refrigerator for 3 hours

Preheat the oven to 350°F.

Heat the oil in a saucepan. Add the onion and cook over medium heat until soft. Place the water, almonds, coriander, cumin, red chilies, and turmeric in a blender and puree. Soak the saffron threads in hot milk for 15 minutes. Stir in the cardamom, cinnamon, peppercorns, bay leaves, and cloves into the onions and cook for 2 minutes. Add the pureed masala and cook for 5–8 minutes, until the oil separates, stirring constantly to prevent the masala from sticking to the bottom of the pan. With a fork, lightly whip the saffron milk into the yogurt and stir into the masala, simmering for 2 minutes.

Set the fish in a casserole dish or deep baking pan and pour the yogurt masala over it, making sure the fish is smothered in sauce. Bake, uncovered, for 15 minutes, until the fish is done, when the sauce starts bubbling. Serve hot with pilao rice or plain rice, chapatis, vegetables, and legumes.

Note: Mughalai pomfret tastes equally delicious barbecued on a grill.

Kerala-Style Fish Curry
(Kerala Min Molee)

A molee is a South Indian preparation in which the food is cooked mainly in coconut milk. In the Orient it is sometimes called a white curry.

Serves 6

3 pounds fresh, cleaned carp or fish of your choice
2 tablespoons coriander seeds
2 dried red chilies, split
1 teaspoon ground turmeric
¼ teaspoon black peppercorns
¼-½ cup coconut liquid
2 tablespoons cider vinegar
¼ cup vegetable oil
1 tablespoon black mustard seeds

1 large red onion, peeled and chopped
8 cloves garlic, peeled
1 1-inch piece fresh gingerroot, peeled and crushed
2 sprigs curry leaves
2 whole dried red chilies
½ tablespoon tamarind concentrate
Salt to taste
1 cup coconut milk (see Index)

Cut the fish into 2-inch pieces. In a small saucepan, roast the coriander, split red chilies, turmeric, and peppercorns. Put the roasted ingredients in a blender with one half of the coconut liquid and the vinegar and puree.

Heat the oil in a large saucepan. Add the mustard seeds and fry over medium heat. When they start popping, add the onion, garlic, ginger, curry leaves, and whole red chilies. Fry until the onion is brown and soft. Add the pureed mixture and fry for 3 minutes. Add the remaining coconut liquid, stirring constantly until the liquid has evaporated. Add the tamarind concentrate, fish, and salt, mixing thoroughly. Simmer for 5 minutes. Pour in the coconut milk, stirring thoroughly. Cook, uncovered, for 5–10 minutes, stirring occasionally to prevent the sauce from sticking to the bottom of the pan. Serve hot with plain rice and Kerala-Style Vegetable Curry (see Index).

South Indian–Style Fish Curry
(Dakshini Min Kari)

Serves 6

3 pounds fresh, cleaned trout or fish of your choice
¼ cup vegetable oil
1 teaspoon black mustard seeds
½ teaspoon fenugreek seeds
2 dried red chilies, crushed
½ teaspoon black peppercorns
1 large onion, peeled and chopped
6 cloves garlic, peeled and chopped
1 1-inch piece fresh gingerroot, peeled and chopped fine
1 teaspoon ground turmeric
Salt to taste
1 cup coconut milk (see Index)
1½ teaspoons tamarind concentrate
¼ cup chopped cilantro leaves

Cut the fish into 2-inch pieces. Heat the oil in a large saucepan. Add the mustard, fenugreek, dried chilies, and peppercorns and fry over medium heat until the mustard seeds start popping. Add the onion, garlic, and ginger and cook until soft. Add the turmeric and salt, stirring for a minute. Mix the coconut milk and tamarind, stirring thoroughly for 5 minutes. Stir in the fish and simmer, uncovered, for 10–15 minutes, stirring occasionally to prevent the sauce from sticking to the bottom of the pan. Garnish with the cilantro leaves and serve hot with plain rice, South Indian Madras-Style Legumes with Vegetables (see Index), and South Indian-Style Green Chutney (see Index).

Hot Goan-Style Fish Curry
(Goa ka Nisteachi Coddi)

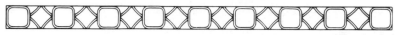

Serves 6

2 large fresh, cleaned pomfrets or
    fish of your choice
½–1 cup coconut liquid
1 teaspoon ground turmeric
4 dried red chilies
¾ cup chopped fresh coconut
1 teaspoon cumin seeds
1 tablespoon coriander seeds
¼ cup vegetable oil
1 large onion, peeled and grated
1 sprig curry leaves
2 large tomatoes
1 teaspoon tamarind concentrate
Salt to taste

Cut the fish into 4-inch pieces. Place the coconut liquid, turmeric, red chilies, coconut, cumin, and coriander seeds in a blender and puree. Heat the oil in a large saucepan. Add the onion and cook over medium heat until browned. Stir in the coconut puree, curry leaves, tomatoes, and tamarind. Cook for 5 minutes, stirring constantly, and add the fish pieces. Mix thoroughly and add salt. Simmer, uncovered, for 10–15 minutes, stirring occasionally, until the fish is done. Serve hot with plain rice, pappadams, and vegetables.

Salmon Curry

(Salmon Machchi Kari)

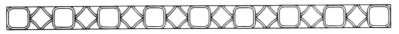

Serves 6

2 pounds fresh salmon steaks
Juice of 1 small lemon
1 teaspoon ground turmeric
Salt to taste
¼ cup vegetable oil
1 large onion, peeled and chopped fine
6 cloves garlic, peeled and crushed
1 1-inch piece fresh gingerroot, peeled and chopped fine

1 teaspoon poppy seeds
¼ teaspoon crushed black peppercorns
1 tablespoon ground coriander
2 teaspoons ground cumin
½ teaspoon ground dried red chilies
1 large tomato, chopped
¼ cup chopped cilantro leaves

Set the salmon steaks on a plate and sprinkle them with the lemon juice, turmeric, and salt. Set aside to marinate for 15 minutes.

Heat the oil in a large saucepan. Add the onion, garlic, and ginger and cook over medium heat until the onion is browned. Mix in the poppy seeds and crushed peppercorns, stirring for a minute. Add the coriander, cumin, and ground chili and cook for 5 minutes, stirring constantly. Add the tomato and mix it into the masala. Add the marinated salmon steaks and lemon juice, gently mixing the masala over the fish. Cover and simmer for 10-15 minutes, until the fish is done.

Garnish with cilantro leaves and serve hot with plain rice, vegetables, Sweet Mango Chutney (see Index), and legumes.

Delicious Shrimp Sautéed in Black Pepper and Mustard Seeds

(Dakshini Prawn Kari)

Serves 6

2 pounds fresh jumbo shrimps
1 teaspoon ground turmeric
Salt to taste
Juice of 1 lemon
¼ cup vegetable oil
1 tablespoon black mustard seeds
1 large onion, peeled and
  chopped fine
6 cloves garlic, peeled and grated
1 1-inch piece fresh gingerroot,
  peeled and chopped fine

2 fresh green chilies, chopped
  fine
½ teaspoon crushed black
  peppercorns
¼ teaspoon ground dried red
  chilies
1 large tomato, peeled and
  chopped
¼ cup chopped cilantro leaves
  (optional)

Shell and devein the shrimps. Transfer them to a large bowl and mix in the turmeric, salt, and lemon juice. Marinate for 15 minutes.

Heat the oil in a large saucepan. Add the mustard seeds and fry over medium heat. When they start popping, add the onion, garlic, ginger, and green chilies and cook for 5 minutes. Stir in the crushed peppercorns and ground chili and mix thoroughly for 2 minutes. Add the tomato and shrimps and stir thoroughly. Reduce the heat, cover, and simmer for 10–15 minutes, until the shrimps are tender and pink, stirring occasionally to prevent the sauce from sticking to the bottom of the pan.

Garnish with cilantro if desired and serve hot with plain rice, chapatis, Sweet Mango Chutney (see Index), and accompanying vegetables.

Hot Malabar-Style Shrimp Curry
(Malabar Prawn Kari)

Serves 6

2 pounds fresh jumbo prawns or shrimps
1 teaspoon tamarind concentrate
2 tablespoons cider vinegar
Salt to taste
1 teaspoon ground turmeric
½–1 cup coconut liquid
¼ cup coriander seeds
2 teaspoons cumin seeds
3 dried red chilies
1 large onion, peeled and chopped
8 cloves garlic, peeled
1 1-inch piece fresh gingerroot, peeled and chopped
¼ teaspoon black peppercorns
¼ cup vegetable oil
1 teaspoon black mustard seeds
½ coconut, shelled and chopped fine
1 cup water
¼ cup chopped cilantro leaves

Shell and devein the shrimps. Soak the tamarind concentrate in the vinegar, salt, and turmeric for 10 minutes. Mix the vinegar mixture with the shrimps and marinate for 30 minutes at room temperature.

Place the coconut liquid, coriander, cumin, chilies, onion, garlic, ginger, and peppercorns in a blender and puree. Heat the oil in a large saucepan. Add the mustard seeds and fry over medium heat. When they start popping, add the chopped coconut and stir for 2 minutes; then stir in the pureed mixture, mixing thoroughly for 8–10 minutes. Add the shrimps and mix thoroughly. Add the water and simmer, uncovered, for 20 minutes, until the shrimps are tender and pink, stirring occasionally to prevent the sauce from sticking to the bottom of the pan.

Garnish with cilantro leaves and serve hot with plain rice, pappadams, chutney, and accompanying vegetables.

My mother, Rajeswari, is an artist and a remarkable human being in addition to being a connoisseur of the different regional foods of India. When her conservative Hindu parents arranged her marriage to my sophisticated father, who at the time was a senior officer in the British Indian Army, my unassuming mother, who had never cooked in her life, had no idea what lay ahead of her. Entertaining and being entertained by maharajas and viceroys of India very quickly forced my mother to learn how to cook and supervise her kitchen staff. I can vividly remember our home in Bangalore overflowing with my parents' hospitality and gracious living to such great artists and philosophers as Ram Gopal and Dr. S. Radhakrishnan. They not only admired my mother, but loved her South Indian cooking preparations, especially her shrimp curries. I recall my father telephoning my mother from his club, all too frequently announcing to her, "I am bringing some friends over for dinner." And always my mother rose to the occasion to serve her guests memorable meals.

Rajeswari's South Indian Shrimp in Fresh Coconut Milk

(Rajeswari's Thankai Riyilu Kari)

This shrimp curry is a favorite of mine and of many others who experienced Rajeswari's extraordinary cuisine.

Serves 6

2 pounds fresh jumbo shrimps, shelled and deveined
1 teaspoon ground turmeric
Salt to taste
¼–½ cup coconut liquid
1 coconut, shelled and chopped
2 tablespoons coriander seeds
3 teaspoons cumin seeds
2 dried red chilies
¼ teaspoon black peppercorns
1 tablespoon black mustard seeds

½ tablespoon tamarind concentrate
1 large red onion, peeled and chopped
6 cloves garlic, peeled
1 1-inch piece fresh gingerroot, peeled and chopped
¼ cup water if needed
¼ cup vegetable oil
2 sprigs curry leaves
¼ cup chopped cilantro leaves

Place the shrimps in a large bowl and mix in the turmeric and salt. Set aside for 10 minutes. Place the coconut liquid, chopped coconut, coriander, cumin, chilies, peppercorns, mustard seeds, tamarind, onion, garlic, and ginger in a blender and puree. Add ¼ cup water if necessary to release the blender blades.

Heat the oil in a large saucepan. Add the pureed mixture and fry over medium heat, stirring constantly, for 8–10 minutes. Stir in the shrimps and curry leaves and mix thoroughly. Simmer, stirring occasionally, for 10 minutes, until the shrimps are tender and pink.

Garnish with cilantro leaves and serve hot with plain basmati rice, chutney, Rajeswari's South Indian Legumes with Vegetables (see Index), and pappadams.

Shrimp in Fresh Coconut Milk
(Jhinga Masala)

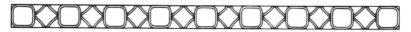

Serves 6

2 pounds fresh jumbo shrimps
¼ cup vegetable oil
1 teaspoon black mustard seeds
¼ teaspoon asafoetida powder
1 large onion, peeled and
    chopped fine
6 cloves garlic, peeled and
    crushed
1 1-inch piece fresh gingerroot,
    peeled and grated fine
1 teaspoon ground turmeric
2 fresh green chilies, cut into thin
    strips
10 curry leaves
2 cups coconut milk (see Index)
Salt to taste

Shell and devein the shrimps. Heat the oil in a large saucepan. Add the mustard seeds and fry over medium heat.
When they start popping, stir in the asafoetida powder for
30 seconds; then add the onion, garlic, and ginger and cook
until the onion is browned. Stir in the turmeric, chilies, and
curry leaves and fry for 2 minutes. Add the coconut milk
and salt, stirring to a simmering point, and add the shrimps.
Mix thoroughly and cook, uncovered, for 15 minutes, until
the shrimps are tender and pink. Serve hot with plain rice,
vegetable sambar, and pappadams.

Madras-Style Shrimp Curry
(Madrasi Yerra Molee)

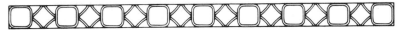

Serves 6

2 pounds fresh jumbo shrimps
1 teaspoon ground turmeric
Salt to taste
¼ coconut, shelled and chopped
2 tablespoons coriander seeds
2 teaspoons cumin seeds
2 dried red chilies
¼ teaspoon fenugreek seeds
1½ teaspoons tamarind
  concentrate
¼–½ cup coconut liquid
¼ cup vegetable oil

1 teaspoon black mustard seeds
¼ teaspoon asafoetida powder
1 large onion, peeled and sliced
  fine
6 cloves garlic, peeled and
  crushed
1 1-inch piece fresh gingerroot,
  peeled and chopped fine
1 fresh green chili, cut into strips
¼ cup plain low-fat yogurt
¼ cup chopped cilantro leaves

Shell and devein the shrimps. Transfer them to a bowl and
mix in the turmeric and salt. Set aside to marinate for 10
minutes. Place the coconut, coriander, cumin, red chilies,
fenugreek, tamarind, and coconut liquid in a blender and
puree. Heat the oil in a large saucepan. Add the mustard
seeds and fry over medium heat. When they start popping,
stir in the asafoetida for 30 seconds; then add the onion,
garlic, ginger, and green chili and cook until the onion is
browned. Add the pureed mixture and the yogurt and cook
for 5-8 minutes until the masala bubbles. Stir in the
shrimps and simmer, uncovered, for 15 minutes, until the
shrimps are tender and pink. Garnish with cilantro leaves
and serve hot with plain rice, pappadams, vegetable sambar,
and chutney.

Hot Coromandel-Style Crab Curry
(Coromandel Mandaraj Kari)

Serves 6

1 coconut, shelled and chopped
¼ cup coriander seeds
¼–½ cup coconut liquid
½–1 cup water
¼ cup vegetable oil
1 tablespoon black mustard seeds
2 dried red chilies
½ teaspoon black peppercorns
6 cloves garlic, peeled and
    crushed
1 1-inch piece fresh gingerroot,
    peeled and chopped fine
1 large red onion, peeled and
    chopped fine
1 teaspoon ground coriander
1 teaspoon ground cumin
Salt to taste
1 teaspoon ground turmeric
⅛ cup ground dried red chilies
¼ cup chopped cilantro leaves
3 pounds fresh crabmeat

To make coconut milk: Place the coconut, coriander seeds, and coconut liquid in a blender and puree. Add ½ cup water if needed to release the blades of the blender. Strain the puree through a cheesecloth. There should be about 1½ cups of coconut milk in the bowl. Blend the puree again with ½ cup water. Strain through a cheesecloth once again and discard the pulp. You should now have 2½ cups of coconut milk.

Heat the oil in a large saucepan. Add the mustard seeds and whole dried red chilies and fry over medium heat. When the mustard seeds start popping, add the peppercorns, garlic, and ginger and fry for 1 minute. Stir in the onion and cook until brown and soft. Add the coriander, cumin, salt, turmeric, and ground chili and cook for 3 minutes. Increase the heat, add the 2½ cups coconut milk, and bring to a boil. Then thoroughly mix in half of the cilantro leaves and the crabmeat. Reduce the heat and simmer, uncovered, for 5 minutes, until the crabmeat is done.

Garnish with the remaining cilantro and serve hot with plain rice, vegetables, and pappadams.

◇ 9 ◇

Vegetable Curries

Spicy Spinach
(Masaledar Sag)

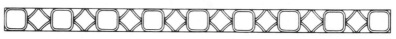

Serves 6

3 pounds fresh spinach leaves, chopped coarse

3 medium turnips, peeled and cut into ½-inch cubes

2 cups water

¼ cup vegetable oil

1 tablespoon black mustard seeds

1 large onion, peeled and chopped fine

6 cloves garlic, peeled and chopped fine

1 1-inch piece fresh gingerroot, peeled and chopped fine

1 teaspoon ground turmeric

½ teaspoon ground dried red chilies

1 tablespoon roasted Basic Garam-Masala (see Index)

Salt to taste

Boil the spinach and turnips in the water in a large saucepan over medium heat for 12–15 minutes, until the vegetables are cooked. Remove and set in a bowl. Mash the vegetables with a fork. Rinse the saucepan and heat the oil in it. Add the mustard seeds and fry over medium heat until they start popping. Stir in the onion, garlic, and ginger and cook until the onion is browned. Add the turmeric, ground chili, garam-masala, and salt, stirring for a minute. Stir in the mashed vegetables. Cover and simmer for 5 minutes, until the liquid evaporates, stirring occasionally to prevent the sauce from sticking to the bottom of the pan.

Serve hot with chapatis, dal, pappadams, and Hot Cilantro Relish (see Index) or with chicken curry.

Mixed Vegetables
(Sabzi Bhaji)

Serves 6

¼ cup vegetable oil
1 tablespoon black mustard seeds
4 cloves garlic, peeled and
  crushed
1 1-inch piece fresh gingerroot,
  peeled and grated
1 teaspoon ground turmeric
¼ teaspoon ground dried red
  chilies
3 medium potatoes, peeled and
  cut into 1-inch cubes
½ pound green beans, sliced
  diagonally into 2-inch strips
3 large carrots, peeled and cut
  into 2-inch strips
½ medium head of cauliflower,
  cut into medium-size pieces
Salt to taste

Heat the oil in a large saucepan. Add the mustard seeds and
fry over medium heat. When they start popping, add the
garlic, ginger, turmeric, and ground chili. Stir thoroughly
for 2 minutes and mix in the vegetables and salt. Cover and
simmer for 10–12 minutes, until the vegetables are done.
Serve hot with rice or chapatis, dal, pappadams, and the
chutney of your choice or with beef curry.

Kerala-Style Vegetable Curry
(Avial)

Serves 6

1 coconut, shelled and chopped
¼–½ cup coconut liquid
¼ cup or more water
1 large onion, peeled and chopped
6 cloves garlic, peeled
1 1½-inch piece fresh gingerroot, peeled and chopped
1½ teaspoon ground turmeric
2 fresh green chilies
1 cup plain low-fat yogurt
1 tablespoon coriander seeds
2 teaspoons cumin seeds
¼ cup vegetable oil
1 tablespoon black mustard seeds

½ pound green beans, cut into 1-inch pieces
½ pound squash, cut into 1-inch pieces
½ pound yams, peeled and cut into 1-inch slices
3 medium-size green bananas, peeled and cut into 1-inch slices
1 large potato, peeled and cut into 1-inch cubes
1 pound pumpkin, peeled and cut into 1-inch slices
Salt to taste
2 sprigs curry leaves (optional)
¼ cup chopped cilantro leaves

Put the coconut and coconut liquid in a blender and blend to a paste. Add water if necessary to release the blades of the blender. Remove and set aside in a bowl. Place ¼ cup water, onion, garlic, ginger, turmeric, chilies, yogurt, coriander, and cumin in the blender and puree.

Heat the oil in a saucepan. Add the mustard seeds. Fry over medium heat. When they start popping, stir in the pureed mixture and fry and brown for 5–8 minutes, stirring constantly. Stir in the beans, squash, yams, bananas, potato, pumpkin, and salt and mix for 5 minutes. Add the coconut paste and mix it into the vegetables. Add the curry leaves. Cover and simmer for 15–20 minutes, until the vegetables are tender.

Curried Mushrooms, Potatoes, and Peas
(Masalewali Alu Mattar Khumben)

Serves 6

¼ cup vegetable oil
1 large onion, peeled and sliced fine
4 cloves garlic, peeled and grated
1 1-inch piece fresh gingerroot, peeled and grated
¼ cup chopped cilantro leaves
1 tablespoon roasted Basic Garam-Masala (see Index)
1 teaspoon ground turmeric

¼ teaspoon ground dried red chilies
2 pounds small potatoes, scrubbed and quartered
Salt to taste
½ cup water
2 pounds fresh mushrooms, cut in half
1 cup shelled fresh or frozen peas

Heat the oil in a large saucepan. Add the onion and fry over medium heat until browned. Stir in the garlic, ginger, and cilantro leaves and fry for 2 minutes. Add the garam-masala, turmeric, and ground chili, stirring for a minute. Stir in the potatoes, salt, and water. Mix thoroughly, cover, and simmer for 8–10 minutes or until the potatoes are three-quarters done, stirring occasionally to prevent the sauce from sticking to the bottom of the pan. Add the mushrooms and peas, mixing them into the potatoes. Cover and cook for 5–8 minutes. Remove the cover, increase the heat, and cook until three-quarters of the liquid has evaporated, stirring the vegetables. Serve hot with rice, chapatis, dal, pappadams, and chutney or with lamb curry.

Bombay-Style Ratatouille
(Bombaiwala Bhartha)

Serves 6

¼ cup vegetable oil
1 large onion, chopped fine
6 cloves garlic, peeled and
crushed
2 fresh green chilies, chopped
fine
1 1-inch piece fresh gingerroot,
peeled and chopped fine
2 tablespoons cider vinegar
2 tablespoons ground coriander
¼ teaspoon ground dried red
chilies
2 teaspoons ground turmeric

3 medium eggplants, cut into
½-inch pieces
1 pound fresh mushrooms,
chopped fine
1 large green bell pepper,
chopped fine
1 pound squash, cut into ¼-inch
pieces
2 turnips, peeled and cut into
¼-inch pieces
5 medium tomatoes, chopped
Salt to taste

Heat the oil in a large saucepan. Add the onion, garlic, green chilies, and ginger and fry over medium heat until the onion is browned. Mix in the vinegar, coriander, ground dried red chilies, and turmeric and stir for 1 minute. Add all the vegetables and the salt and mix thoroughly. Cover and simmer for 15 minutes, until the vegetables are cooked. Remove the lid, increase the heat, and cook until the liquid evaporates, stirring constantly to prevent the vegetables from sticking to the bottom of the pan. Serve hot with chicken curry and rice.

Green Beans Sautéed with Coconut

(Sem aur Nariyal ki Sabzi)

Serves 6

¼ cup vegetable oil
1 tablespoon black mustard seeds
4 dried red chilies
Pinch of asafoetida
2 medium onions, peeled and
    chopped
1 ½-inch piece fresh gingerroot,
    peeled and chopped fine
4 cloves garlic, peeled and
    crushed
3 pounds green beans, cut into 1-
    inch pieces
½ cup coarsely grated coconut
Salt to taste

Heat the oil in a large saucepan. Add the mustard seeds and fry over medium heat until they start popping. Add the red chilies and asafoetida and stir for 30 seconds; stir in the onions, ginger, and garlic and cook until browned. Mix in the green beans, coconut, and salt. Cover and simmer for 8–10 minutes or until the beans are cooked. Remove the lid, increase the heat, and cook for 5 minutes, until the water evaporates. Serve hot with plain rice, chapatis, or any curry entrée.

Curried Cauliflower and Peas
(Masalewali Gobi aur Mattar)

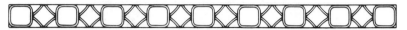

Serves 6

¼ cup vegetable oil
1 tablespoon black mustard seeds
1 teaspoon cumin seeds
1 medium onion, peeled and
    grated
4 cloves garlic, peeled and
    crushed
1 1-inch piece fresh gingerroot,
    peeled and grated
1 fresh green chili, grated
1 teaspoon ground turmeric
¼ teaspoon ground dried red
    chilies
1 large head of cauliflower, cut
    into 1-inch pieces
2 cups shelled fresh or frozen
    peas
Salt to taste

Heat the oil in a large saucepan. Add the mustard and
cumin seeds and fry over medium heat until the mustard
seeds start popping. Stir in the onion, garlic, ginger, and
green chili and fry until browned. Add the turmeric and
ground chili and stir for 30 seconds. Mix in the cauliflower,
peas, and salt. Cover and simmer for 8–10 minutes, until
the vegetables are done, stirring occasionally to prevent the
sauce from sticking to the bottom of the pan. Serve hot with
pooris, rice, and chicken curry.

Eggplant in Cream Sauce

(Baigan ka Bhartha)

Serves 6

4 medium eggplants, cut into
2-inch slices
1 quart water
Salt to taste
¼ cup vegetable oil
1 tablespoon black mustard
seeds
1 large onion, peeled and
chopped fine
6 cloves garlic, peeled and
crushed

1 cinnamon stick
¼ teaspoon black peppercorns
1 1½-inch piece fresh gingerroot,
peeled and sliced into thin
strips
2 fresh green chilies, chopped
fine
1 tablespoon ground coriander
2 teaspoons ground cumin
1 teaspoon ground turmeric
¼ cup sour cream

Put the eggplant in a large pot with the water and salt.
Cover and boil over medium heat about 10 minutes, until
the eggplant is tender. Remove the lid and increase the heat;
cook until the water evaporates. Mash the eggplant with a
fork and set aside.

Heat the oil in a large saucepan. Add the mustard seeds.
When they start to pop, add the onion, garlic, cinnamon,
peppercorns, ginger, and green chilies and fry over medium
heat, stirring occasionally, until the onion is browned. Mix
in the coriander, cumin, and turmeric and stir for 3–4
minutes, until the oil separates. Add the mashed eggplant
and mix thoroughly. Mix the sour cream into the eggplant.
Cover and simmer for 5 minutes.

Serve hot with plain rice, chapatis, and any nonvegetarian entrée if desired.

Fresh Vegetables and Indian Cheese
(Sabzi Paneer)

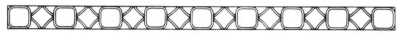

Serves 6

8 cups milk
4 tablespoons fresh lemon juice
1 pound fresh mushrooms, sliced
    fine
2½ cups water
¼ cup vegetable oil
1 large onion, peeled and
    chopped fine
6 cloves garlic, peeled and
    chopped fine
1 1-inch piece fresh gingerroot,
    peeled and chopped fine
2 fresh green chilies, chopped fine
1 tablespoon ground coriander
2 teaspoons cumin seeds
1 teaspoon ground turmeric
¼ teaspoon crushed black
    peppercorns
¼ teaspoon ground dried red
    chilies
1 teaspoon paprika
1 tablespoon Basic Garam-Masala
    (see Index)
1 large tomato, chopped
1 medium head of cauliflower, cut
    into 1-inch pieces
2 large potatoes, peeled and cut
    into ½-inch pieces
2 cups shelled fresh or frozen peas
Salt to taste
¼ cup cilantro leaves

To make the Indian Cheese (paneer): In a large pot, boil the milk over medium heat. Gently stir in the lemon juice and mix for 10 seconds until the milk curdles and separates from the yellowish whey. The curds should be in lumps. Pour the curdled milk into a large cheesecloth, twist, and strain over sink. Hang the cheesecloth over the sink for 45 minutes until all the liquid has drained. Compress the cheese for 3 hours under the weight of a heavy object or chopping board to flatten it out.

Remove the weight and the cheese from the cheesecloth.

Cut the Indian Cheese into ½- by ½- by 1-inch pieces and set aside. Boil the mushrooms in ½ cup of the water in a small pot for 5 minutes. Drain and set aside. Heat the oil in a large saucepan. Add the cheese pieces and fry gently over medium heat for 5 minutes, until golden brown on both sides. Remove the cheese and drain on paper towels. Add the onion, garlic, ginger, and green chilies to the oil and brown for 5–7 minutes, stirring constantly. Stir in the coriander, cumin, turmeric, peppercorns, ground chili, paprika, and garam-masala and fry for 3–5 minutes, stirring constantly. Add the tomato and mix and cook for 5–8 minutes, until soft and the oil separates from the masala.

Thoroughly mix in the vegetables (except the mushrooms), the rest of the water, and salt. Cover and simmer for 8–12 minutes, until the vegetables are done, stirring occasionally to prevent the sauce from sticking to the bottom of the pan. Add the mushrooms and fried cheese, stirring gently.

Garnish with cilantro leaves and serve hot with pooris, pilao rice, lamb curry, Sweet Mango Chutney (see Index), and pappadams.

Mughal-Style Vegetables in Delicate Almond Cardamom Sauce

(Mughalai Sabzi Korma)

Serves 6

1 recipe Indian Cheese (see Index)
½ teaspoon saffron threads
¼ cup hot milk
2 cups water
¼ cup blanched almonds
1 large onion, peeled and chopped
6 cloves garlic, peeled
1 1-inch piece fresh gingerroot, peeled and chopped
2 fresh green chilies
¼ teaspoon ground nutmeg
1 teaspoon ground turmeric
1 teaspoon paprika
½ teaspoon ground dried red chilies
1 tablespoon Mughal-Style Garam-Masala (see Index)
¼ cup vegetable oil

12 green cardamom pods
1 cinnamon stick
½ teaspoon whole cloves
½ teaspoon black peppercorns
4 bay leaves
2 large tomatoes, cut into medium-size pieces
2 large potatoes, peeled and cut into 1-inch pieces
2 large carrots, peeled and cut into 1-inch pieces
1 small head of cauliflower, cut into 1-inch pieces
2 cups shelled peas
1 pound fresh mushrooms, cut in half
Salt to taste
¼ cup sour cream
1 cup plain low-fat yogurt
¼ cup chopped cilantro leaves

Cut the Indian Cheese into ½- by ½- by 1-inch pieces and set aside. Soak the saffron threads in the hot milk for 15 minutes and set aside. Place ½ cup of the water, the almonds, onion, garlic, ginger, green chilies, nutmeg, turmeric, paprika, ground chili, and garam-masala in a blender and puree. Heat the oil in a large saucepan. Add the cheese pieces and fry over medium heat for 5 minutes, until golden brown on both sides. Remove the cheese and drain on paper towels.

Add the cardamom, cinnamon, cloves, peppercorns, and bay leaves to the oil and fry for 2–3 minutes, until the spices turn a shade darker. Add the pureed mixture and fry for 8–10 minutes, stirring constantly, until the oil separates. Add the tomatoes and cook for 3–5 minutes, until soft. Mix in the vegetables and salt and stir thoroughly for 5 minutes. With a fork, lightly whip the sour cream into the yogurt and pour the mixture over the vegetables. Add the remaining water, cover, and simmer for 10–12 minutes, until the vegetables are done. Pour the saffron milk over the vegetables and gently add the Indian Cheese, stirring thoroughly. Cover and cook for 5 minutes.

Garnish with cilantro leaves and serve hot with pilao rice, nan roti, dal, and any nonvegetarian entrée.

Okra in Cumin and Garlic
(Bhindi Masala)

Serves 6

¼ cup vegetable oil
1 large onion, peeled and
    chopped fine
10 cloves garlic, peeled and
    crushed
2 fresh green chilies, chopped
    fine
1 teaspoon ground turmeric
1 tablespoon ground cumin
3 pounds okra
Salt to taste

Heat the oil in a large saucepan. Add the onion, garlic, and
green chilies and fry over medium heat until browned. Stir
in the turmeric and cumin and fry for 2 minutes, until the
oil separates. Mix in the okra and salt. Cover, reduce the
heat, and simmer for 8–10 minutes, until the okra is tender,
stirring occasionally to prevent the onion and spices from
sticking to the bottom of the pan. Serve hot with chapatis or
plain rice and any nonvegetarian curry if desired.

Benares-Style Cauliflower and Potatoes
(Rasedar Benaresi Alu-Gobi)

Serves 6

1 cup water
1 large onion, peeled and
chopped
6 cloves garlic, peeled
1 ½-inch piece fresh gingerroot,
peeled and chopped
1 tablespoon coriander seeds
¼ cup vegetable oil
1 teaspoon cumin seeds
1 teaspoon caraway seeds
1 tablespoon Basic Garam-Masala
(see Index)
1 teaspoon ground turmeric
1 large head of cauliflower, cut
into 1-inch pieces
2 large potatoes, peeled and cut
into 1-inch cubes
Salt to taste

Place ¼ cup of the water, the onion, garlic, ginger, and coriander seeds in a blender and puree. Heat the oil in a large saucepan. Add the cumin and caraway seeds and fry over medium heat for 1–2 minutes. Add the pureed mixture, stirring for 6–8 minutes, until the oil separates. Mix in the garam-masala and turmeric and stir for 30 seconds. Add the cauliflower, potatoes, salt, and remaining water. Cover and simmer for 8–10 minutes, until the vegetables are done, stirring occasionally to prevent the sauce from sticking to the bottom of the pan. Serve hot with pooris, chapatis or plain rice, dal, and mango chutney.

◇ **10** ◇

Curries in a Hurry

Fragrant Indian Meatballs
(Kofta)

Serves 4

1 pound lean ground beef
1 medium onion, peeled and
chopped fine
3 cloves garlic, peeled and
crushed
1 ½-inch piece fresh gingerroot,
peeled and chopped fine
1 fresh green chili, chopped fine
½ teaspoon roasted Basic Garam-
Masala (see Index)
2 tablespoons plain low-fat yogurt
1 tablespoon finely chopped
cilantro or fresh mint leaves

Salt to taste
1 teaspoon turmeric
2 tablespoons vegetable oil
1 cinnamon stick
3 green cardamom pods
6 cloves
10 black peppercorns
2 bay leaves
1 medium tomato, chopped
1 cup water

In a bowl, thoroughly mix the meat, onion, garlic, ginger, green chili, garam-masala, yogurt, cilantro or mint, salt, and turmeric. Divide into 12 medium-sized balls and set aside.

Heat the oil in a large saucepan. Add the cinnamon, cardamom, cloves, peppercorns, and bay leaves and fry over medium heat until the spices turn a shade darker. Add the meatballs, stir gently, and fry for 5 minutes, until evenly browned. Stir in the tomato and water. Cover and simmer for 15 minutes, until the meatballs are cooked through.

Serve hot with plain rice, Sweet Mango Chutney (see Index), accompanying vegetables, and pappadams.

Fried Beef

(Bhuna Gosht)

Serves 6

2 pounds lean beef stew meat, cut into 1-inch cubes
½ teaspoon ground turmeric
1 tablespoon cider vinegar
2 tablespoons vegetable oil
6 cloves garlic, peeled and minced fine
1 large onion, peeled and minced fine
1 fresh green chili, minced fine
1 ¼-inch piece fresh gingerroot, peeled and minced fine
1 tablespoon Basic Curry Powder (see Index)
1 tablespoon dried or freshly grated coconut
Salt to taste
1 large tomato, chopped

Preheat the oven to 400°F.

Remove and discard any fat from the meat. Set the meat in a flat dish and mix in the turmeric and vinegar. Set aside for 10 minutes.

Heat the oil in a large saucepan. Add the garlic, onion, green chili, and ginger and fry over medium heat until the onion is browned. Stir in the curry powder and coconut and fry for 3-4 minutes, stirring occasionally, until the oil separates. Add the meat and vinegar, salt, and the tomato, mix thoroughly, increase the heat, and fry for 3-4 minutes.

Transfer the meat mixture to a casserole dish. Cover tightly with aluminum foil and the lid. Bake for 30 minutes. Reduce the heat to 300°F and bake for 15 minutes, until the meat is tender.

Serve hot with plain rice or chapatis and accompanying vegetables and salad.

Bell Peppers Stuffed with Ground Meat and Fresh Mint

(Masaledar Kheema Pudina)

Serves 4

4 large green bell peppers
2 pounds lean ground lamb,
  beef, pork, or turkey
1 large onion, peeled and
  chopped fine
5 cloves garlic, peeled and
  crushed
1 ¼-inch piece fresh gingerroot,
  peeled and chopped fine
10–12 blanched almonds, ground
1 fresh green chili, chopped fine
Salt to taste

2 tablespoons fresh mint leaves
¼ cup vegetable oil
4 green cardamom pods
1 cinnamon stick
6 cloves
¼ teaspoon black peppercorns
2 bay leaves
1 teaspoon ground coriander
1 teaspoon cumin seeds
½ teaspoon ground turmeric
1 teaspoon Basic Garam-Masala
  (see Index)

Slice off the cap at the top of the bell peppers and scoop out the seeds. In a large bowl, mix the meat, half of the onion, half of the garlic, half of the ginger, the almonds, green chili, salt, and mint leaves. Preheat the oven to 400°F.

Heat the oil in a saucepan. Add the cardamom, cinnamon, cloves, peppercorns, and bay leaves and fry over medium heat until the spices turn a shade darker. Add the remaining onion, garlic, and ginger and stir for 2 minutes. Mix in the coriander, cumin, turmeric, and garam-masala and stir for a minute. Add the meat mixture, mix thoroughly, cover, and simmer for 10 minutes, stirring occasionally to prevent the ingredients from sticking to the bottom of the pan.

Remove and cool. Remove the bay leaves, cinnamon, cardamom pods, peppercorns, and cloves from the meat mixture.

Stuff the bell peppers with the meat mixture and place them in a lightly greased deep casserole dish. Reduce the heat to 300°F, cover the casserole dish, and bake for 10 minutes. Serve hot with plain rice, legumes, and chutney.

Ground Meat with Peas

(Kheema Mattar Masala)

Serves 4

2 tablespoons vegetable oil
¼ teaspoon crushed black
  peppercorns
1 small onion, peeled and minced
  fine
3 cloves garlic, peeled and minced
  fine
1 tablespoon Basic Curry Powder
  (see Index)
3 medium tomatoes, chopped
1 pound lean ground lamb or beef
2 tablespoons chopped fresh mint
  leaves
1 tablespoon plain low-fat yogurt
Salt to taste
1 10-ounce package frozen peas

Heat the oil in a medium saucepan. Add the crushed peppercorns and fry for 30 seconds. Add the onion and garlic and
fry over medium heat until browned. Stir in the curry
powder and fry for a minute. Add the tomatoes and cook for
2–3 minutes, until soft. Add the meat, mint leaves, yogurt,
and salt, stirring thoroughly. Cover and simmer for 10
minutes. Stir in the frozen peas, cover, and cook for another
5 minutes. Serve hot with plain rice, Sweet Mango Chutney
(see Index), salad, and pappadams.

Ground Meat with Peas and Potatoes

(Alu-Kheema-Mattar)

Serves 4

2 tablespoons vegetable oil
1 medium onion, peeled and
  chopped fine
5 cloves garlic, peeled and
  chopped fine
1 ½-inch piece fresh gingerroot,
  peeled and chopped fine
1 fresh green chili, chopped fine
½ teaspoon ground turmeric
1 teaspoon ground coriander
1 teaspoon ground cumin

1 teaspoon Basic Garam-Masala
  (see Index)
2 pounds lean ground lamb,
  beef, pork, or turkey
3 medium potatoes, peeled and
  quartered
Salt to taste
1 large tomato, chopped
1 10-ounce package frozen peas
2 tablespoons chopped cilantro
  leaves

Heat the oil in a large saucepan. Add the onion, garlic, ginger, and green chili and fry over medium heat until browned. Stir in the turmeric, coriander, cumin, and garam-masala and fry for a minute. Add the ground meat, potatoes, salt, and tomato and stir thoroughly. Cover and simmer for 15–20 minutes, stirring occasionally to prevent the ingredients from sticking to the bottom of the pan. Add the peas and cilantro and mix thoroughly. Cover and cook for about 5 minutes. Serve hot with chapatis or plain rice, legumes, and chutney.

Curried Ground Meat with Eggplant
(Masala Kheema-Baigan)

Serves 4

1 medium eggplant
¼ cup vegetable oil
1 cinnamon stick
6 green cardamom pods
2 bay leaves
½ teaspoon black peppercorns
¼ teaspoon whole cloves
1 medium onion, peeled and grated
4 cloves garlic, peeled and crushed

1 ½-inch piece fresh gingerroot, peeled and grated
1 fresh green chili, grated
1 tablespoon Basic Curry Powder (see Index)
1 large tomato, chopped
2 pounds ground lamb, beef, pork, or turkey
Salt to taste

Cut the eggplant into 2-inch strips. Heat the oil in a large saucepan. Add the cinnamon, cardamom, bay leaves, peppercorns, and cloves and fry over medium heat until the spices turn a shade darker. Add the onion, garlic, ginger, and green chili, stirring occasionally until the onion is golden brown. Stir in the curry powder and fry for a minute. Add the tomato and cook for a minute, until soft. Add the meat and salt, mixing thoroughly. Cover and simmer for 10 minutes, stirring occasionally to prevent the ingredients from sticking to the bottom of the pan. Add the eggplant and mix thoroughly. Cover and cook for another 7–10 minutes, stirring occasionally. Serve hot with rice or chapatis, dal, and chutney.

Indian Hamburger

(Kheema Tikka)

Serves 6

2 pounds lean ground lamb or beef
1 egg
2 tablespoons bread crumbs
1 medium onion, peeled and chopped fine
3 cloves garlic, peeled and chopped fine
1 ½-inch piece fresh gingerroot, peeled and chopped fine
¼ cup chopped cilantro or fresh mint leaves
¼ teaspoon crushed black peppercorns
¼ teaspoon ground black mustard seeds
Salt to taste
2 tablespoons vegetable oil

In a large bowl, thoroughly mix all of the ingredients except the oil. Divide the mixture into six equal hamburger patties. Heat the oil in a large saucepan. Add the hamburgers and cook over medium heat until browned. Turn the patties and cook until browned on the other side and done to your taste. Serve on warm wheat buns or with chapatis and Hot Cilantro Relish (see Index) or Sweet Mint Chutney (see Index) and salad.

Chicken Curry
(Masaledar Murgh)

Serves 4

1 2-pound chicken
¼ cup vegetable oil
4 green cardamom pods
2 bay leaves
1 cinnamon stick
4 cloves
¼ teaspoon black peppercorns
2 medium onions, peeled and sliced fine
5 cloves garlic, peeled and chopped fine

1 ½-inch piece fresh gingerroot, peeled and chopped fine
1 fresh green chili, chopped fine
1 tablespoon ground coriander
1 teaspoon ground turmeric
1 teaspoon ground cumin
⅛ teaspoon ground dried red chilies
Salt to taste
2 cups water

Remove the fat and skin from the chicken and cut into 8 serving pieces. Heat the oil in a large saucepan. Add the cardamom, bay leaves, cinnamon, cloves, and peppercorns and fry over medium heat until the spices turn a shade darker. Add the onions, garlic, ginger, and green chili and fry until golden brown, stirring occasionally. Stir in the coriander, turmeric, cumin, and ground chili and cook for 2 minutes. Add the chicken pieces and salt and stir thoroughly. Pour in the water, cover, and simmer for 20–30 minutes, until the chicken is tender, stirring occasionally to prevent the sauce from sticking to the bottom of the pan. Serve hot with plain rice, vegetables, and Hot Cilantro Relish (see Index).

Curried Shrimp
(Masalewale Jhinga)

Serves 4

Juice of 1 small lemon
1 pound medium-size shelled and
   deveined shrimps
2 tablespoons vegetable oil
1 teaspoon black mustard seeds
¼ teaspoon fenugreek seeds
1 large onion, peeled and
   chopped
5 cloves garlic, peeled and
   crushed
½ teaspoon ground turmeric
¼ teaspoon ground dried red
   chilies
½ cup dried shredded coconut
2 tablespoons plain low-fat yogurt
Salt to taste

In a small bowl, squeeze the lemon juice over the shrimps
and set aside. Heat the oil in a medium saucepan. Add the
mustard and fenugreek seeds and fry over medium heat.
When the mustard seeds start popping, add the onion and
fry until golden brown, stirring occasionally. Add the garlic,
turmeric, ground chili, coconut, and yogurt and mix thoroughly for 1–2 minutes. Add the shrimps and salt and stir.
Reduce the heat, cover, and cook for 10 minutes, until the
shrimps are cooked, stirring occasionally to prevent the
ingredients from sticking to the bottom of the pan. Serve
hot with plain rice, zucchini, Hot Cilantro Relish (see
Index), and pappadams.

Mixed Vegetable Curry
(Bhaji)

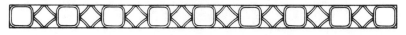

Serves 4

¼ cup vegetable oil
1 medium onion, peeled and
  chopped
4 cloves garlic, peeled and
  chopped
1 ½-inch piece fresh gingerroot,
  peeled and chopped
1 fresh green chili
1 cinnamon stick
1 tablespoon Basic Curry
  Powder (see Index)
½ teaspoon ground turmeric

1 large potato, peeled and cut
  into ½-inch cubes
1 pound broccoli, cut into
  1-inch spears
2 large carrots, peeled and cut
  diagonally into 2-inch strips
1 small head of cauliflower, cut
  into 1-inch flowerets
1 large tomato, chopped
Salt to taste
1 cup water

Heat the oil in a large saucepan. Add the onion, garlic, ginger, green chili, and cinnamon and fry over medium heat until the onion is browned. Mix in the curry powder and turmeric and stir for 1–2 minutes. Add the potato, broccoli, carrots, cauliflower, tomato, and salt and mix thoroughly. Pour in the water, cover, and simmer for 10–12 minutes, until the vegetables are done, stirring occasionally to prevent the ingredients from sticking to the bottom of the pan. Serve hot with chapatis or plain rice, dal, and chutney.

◇ 11 ◇

Sumptuous Pilao and Rice Dishes

Cooking Plain Basmati Rice

The Indians have, over 5,000 years, mastered the art of cooking rice to a perfection that is not seen anywhere else in the world. I cook plain basmati rice in the following simple way, and 10 times out of 10, the end result is perfect:

1. Soak the rice in water for at least 15–20 minutes. To soak the rice, always add twice the amount of water as of rice.
2. Wash the rice two or three times in cold water only, so as to retain its nutrients.
3. If you are cooking 1 cup of plain basmati rice, boil 1 quart of water in a medium pot over high heat. Reduce the heat to medium and add 1 teaspoon of vegetable oil so that the rice does not stick to the bottom of the pot and each grain of rice turns out fluffy and tender and not mushy and lumpy. Add the rice and cook for only 5 minutes, stirring occasionally. At the end of 5 minutes the rice should be three-quarters cooked.
4. Preheat the oven to 400°F.
5. Drain the rice in a colander and run cold water over the rice for 2 or 3 seconds. Let the rice sit in the colander for at least 5 minutes so all the water has drained.
6. Place the partially cooked rice back in the pot, cover, and bake for 5–8 minutes. Reduce the oven heat to 300°F.
7. Bake about 8 minutes, until the rice is cooked and fluffy. Serve hot with curry and accompanying entrées.

India is known to have traded in diamonds as early as 800 B.C. and may have done so long before that. In addition to the famous Koh-i-noor diamond, most of the diamonds of the European crown jewels were taken from India. In fact nearly all of the famous historical diamonds were found in India, which is probably why precious stones have played an important role in the traditions, mythologies, legends, and poems of the Hindus.

One of the famous crown diamonds, the Orloff "brilliant," has its own strange story. It is a beautiful stone of 199.6 carats and came from the state of Carnatic, in South India. It is considered to be of the most superb quality and retains its original Indian cutting. It was named after Prince Gregori Orloff, one of the lovers of Catherine the Great of Russia. The diamond was first heard of as one of the eyes of a statue of Brahma in a temple (between Madras and Mysore) on the fortified island of Srirangam on the river Kaveri, two miles north of Trichinopoly in Mysore. One stormy monsoon night a deserter from the French garrison in India, after years of planning and scheming, stole one of the diamonds right out of Brahma's eye, swam across the swollen river, and escaped through the jungles of Mysore to Madras. There he sold it for $10,000 to an English sea captain, who secretly disposed of it in London for $60,000. In 1774 it was sold in Amsterdam to Prince Orloff for $450,000, to be paid for over many years. Prince Orloff had lost his boudoir favors with the amorous Catherine and presented the glittering stone to her in an effort both to improve his fortunes and to regain his bedroom privileges. Catherine, who was also a famous collector of jewels, accepted Orloff's precious gift and gave him a marble palace in St. Petersburg (Leningrad) but did not restore him to his former graces with her. Catherine had the stone mounted in the Romanoff scepter, and today it is one of the most valuable treasures of the Diamond Fund in the Kremlin.

Carnatic (Mysore)-Style Lamb Pilao Rice

(Karnataka Pilao)

Trichinopoly was part of the Carnatic empire of Muhammad Ali Khan, nawab of Carnatic (1750–95), whose chefs made this dish with the delicately perfumed spices of the Carnatic region.

Serves 6

Lamb

2½ pounds boneless leg of lamb, cut into 1-inch cubes
2 cups plain low-fat yogurt
Salt to taste
¼ cup water
1 teaspoon ground turmeric
1 teaspoon paprika
8 green cardamom pods, pods removed and discarded
1 cinnamon stick, broken into small pieces
8 cloves
1½ tablespoons ground coriander
1 tablespoon ground cumin
¼ teaspoon ground nutmeg
¼ teaspoon ground mace
¼ teaspoon ground dried red chilies
10 cloves garlic, peeled and chopped
1 2-inch piece fresh gingerroot, peeled and chopped
3 fresh green chilies
¼ cup cilantro leaves
½ cup vegetable oil
8 medium onions, peeled and sliced

Rice

2 pounds (4 cups) long-grain basmati rice, soaked in cold water for 20 minutes
1 teaspoon saffron threads
¼ cup hot milk
2½ quarts water
1 tablespoon vegetable oil
8 cloves
4 black cardamom pods
1 cinnamon stick
½ teaspoon black peppercorns
Salt to taste
¼ cup raisins
3 large potatoes, peeled and cut into ½-inch cubes

Prepare the lamb: Remove any fat from the meat. Place the meat in a bowl and add the yogurt and salt, mix, and set aside. Place the water, turmeric, paprika, cardamom, cinnamon, cloves, coriander, cumin, nutmeg, mace, ground chili, garlic, ginger, green chilies, and cilantro in a blender and puree. In a large bowl, mix the puree with the meat, yogurt, and salt and set aside. Heat the oil in a large saucepan. Add the onions and fry over medium heat until browned but crisp. Remove the onions and drain on paper towels. When cool, crush the onions and set aside. Mix ½ cup of the crushed onions with 2 tablespoons of the oil from the pan with the marinated meat and set aside for 3 hours. In the same large saucepan that the onions were cooked in, heat the oil and add the meat and marinade and boil. Reduce to medium heat, cover, and cook for 1 hour, stirring occasionally to prevent the masala from sticking to the bottom of the pan, until the meat is tender and the curry masala is thick. Remove from heat and set aside.

Prepare the rice: Wash and drain the rice in a colander. Preheat the oven to 450°F. Soak the saffron threads in the hot milk for 15 minutes. Place the water in a large pot and boil the rice with the oil, cloves, cardamom, cinnamon, peppercorns, and salt over medium heat for 3–4 minutes, until half done. Drain the rice in a colander.

Assemble the dish: Grease a large deep casserole dish with oil and spread the marinated meat, raisins, and potatoes in the dish. Sprinkle 2 tablespoons of the saffron milk and half the crushed browned onions over the meat. Evenly spread on the rice and sprinkle the rice with the remaining milk and browned onions. Seal the dish tightly with aluminum foil and the lid. Place in the center of the oven and cook for 30 minutes. Reduce the heat to 300°F and cook for 45 minutes, until the meat is tender. Turn off the heat and keep the pilao in the oven for another 5–8 minutes. Serve hot with pappadams and tomato chutney.

Rajeswari's Hyderabad-Style Lamb Pilao Rice

(Rajeswari ki Hyderabadi Pilao)

My mother, Raja Rajeswari, was born in Andhra Pradesh, South India, which was at one time part of the kingdom of Golconda. Her fame as a chef was well known not only among her and my father's circle of friends, but with our school friends and teachers as well. Her cooking style was influenced by Mughal cuisine. My mother taught this particular recipe for pilao rice to our chef, Shafi, who mastered it and prepared it every Sunday for 20 years for our special guests. Luncheon, which began at around two in the afternoon, was usually accompanied by music and served under a colorful shamiana (tent) on our front lawns. After a fifteen-course Indian feast the guests left at around six or seven in the evening, immensely satisfied.

Serves 6

2 pounds boneless leg of lamb, cut into 1-inch cubes
1 cup plain low-fat yogurt
1 teaspoon ground turmeric
¼ teaspoon ground dried red chilies
Salt to taste
5 cups water
½ coconut, shelled and chopped
1 large onion, peeled and chopped fine
6 cloves garlic, peeled and chopped fine
1 ½-inch piece fresh gingerroot, peeled and chopped fine

2 fresh green chilies, chopped fine
1 tablespoon Basic Garam-Masala (see Index)
¼ teaspoon ground nutmeg
1 tablespoon coriander seeds
2 teaspoons cumin seeds
¼ cup vegetable oil
6 green cardamom pods
3 black cardamom pods
2 cinnamon sticks
½ teaspoon black peppercorns
¼ teaspoon whole cloves
3 bay leaves

2 medium potatoes, peeled and
cut into ½-inch cubes

4 cups long-grain basmati rice,
soaked in cold water for 20
minutes

1 cup shelled fresh peas *or* 1 10-
ounce package frozen peas

¼ cup finely chopped fresh mint
leaves

¼ cup cilantro leaves, chopped
fine

Remove any fat from the meat and place the meat in a large bowl. Mix in the yogurt, turmeric, ground chili, and salt. Place ½ cup of the water, the chopped coconut, onion, garlic, ginger, green chilies, garam-masala, nutmeg, coriander, and cumin seeds in a blender and puree. Add more water if needed to release the blades of the blender.

Heat the oil in a large saucepan. Add the cardamom, cinnamon, peppercorns, cloves, and bay leaves and fry over medium heat until the spices turn a shade darker. Mix in the pureed mixture and stir constantly for 8–10 minutes, until the oil separates. Add the meat and the yogurt marinade. Mix thoroughly, cover, and simmer for 30 minutes, stirring occasionally to prevent the sauce from sticking to the bottom of the pan. Add the potatoes and mix thoroughly. Turn off the heat.

Preheat the oven to 400°F.

Wash the rice and boil it in 2½ quarts water over medium heat for 5 minutes, until half done. Remove and drain in a colander. Mix in the peas and set aside.

Transfer the meat mixture to a large casserole and sprinkle with mint and cilantro leaves. Spread on the rice. Cover the dish tightly with aluminum foil and the lid. Bake for 15 minutes. Reduce the heat to 300°F and bake for 20 minutes. Turn off the heat and leave the casserole in the oven for another 5 minutes.

Remove and transfer to a serving platter. Serve hot with pappadams, spinach, dal, and mango chutney.

yderabad-Style Chicken Pilao Rice
(Hyderabadi Murgh Pilao)

This recipe comes from the kitchens of the once splendid court of Golconda, the kingdom where diamonds were once mined.

Serves 6

Chicken

2½ pounds chicken breasts, legs, and thighs
¼ cup vegetable oil
1 large onion, peeled and chopped fine
6 cloves garlic, peeled and chopped fine
1 1-inch piece fresh gingerroot, peeled and chopped fine
12 green cardamom pods
24 cloves

5 bay leaves
½ teaspoon black peppercorns
1 cinnamon stick
¼ teaspoon ground nutmeg
1 tablespoon ground coriander
¼ teaspoon ground dried red chilies
¼ cup sour cream
1 cup plain low-fat yogurt
Salt to taste

Rice

2 cups long-grain basmati rice
¼ cup vegetable oil
1 large onion, peeled and chopped fine

¼ cup blanched almonds
½ cup raisins

Prepare the chicken: Remove the skin and fat from the chicken. Heat the oil in a large saucepan. Add the onion, garlic, and ginger and fry over medium heat until browned. Add the cardamom, cloves, bay leaves, peppercorns, and cinnamon and stir for 3–4 minutes. Stir in the nutmeg, coriander, and ground chili and cook for 2 minutes. With a fork, lightly whip the sour cream into the yogurt and pour over the spice mixture. Stir thoroughly for 2–3 minutes and add the chicken pieces. Mix the sauce into the chicken, add salt, and stir thoroughly. Reduce the heat, cover, and cook for 20–25 minutes, until the chicken is tender, stirring occasionally to prevent the sauce from sticking to the bottom of the pan. Turn off the heat and set aside.

Prepare the rice: Prepare Plain Basmati Rice (see Index), adjusting the quantities for 2 cups rice, and set aside. Heat the oil in a small saucepan. Add the onion and fry over medium heat until browned but crisp. Remove the onion and drain on paper towels. Add the blanched almonds and raisins to the pan and fry until the almonds are golden brown and the raisins are puffed up. Remove and drain on paper towels.

Assemble the dish: Preheat the oven to 300°F. Place the chicken in a large casserole dish. Add the rice and spread it carefully over the chicken. Garnish with the browned onions, almonds, and raisins. Cover the dish tightly with aluminum foil and the lid. Bake for 15 minutes. Turn off the heat and leave the casserole in the oven for 10 minutes more.

Serve hot with vegetables, mint chutney, and pappadams.

Emperor's Kashmir-Style Chicken Pilao Rice
(Kashmiri Padshahi Murgh Pilao)

This pilao dish is representative of Kashmir today as it was during the reign of Shah Jahan (1628–58).

Serves 6

1 3-pound chicken
3 quarts water
¼ cup unsalted pistachios
2 teaspoons fennel seeds
2 tablespoons cumin seeds
1 teaspoon paprika
1 tablespoon Kashmir-Style
    Garam-Masala (see Index)
¼ cup plain low-fat yogurt
1 teaspoon saffron threads
¼ cup hot milk
5 tablespoons vegetable oil
2 large onions, peeled and
    chopped fine
¼ cup blanched almonds

½ cup raisins
3 black cardamom pods
6 green cardamom pods
2 cinnamon sticks
½ teaspoon whole cloves
3 bay leaves
½ teaspoon black peppercorns
¼ teaspoon ground nutmeg
6 cloves garlic, peeled and
    chopped fine
Salt to taste
¼ cup fresh mint leaves
3 cups long-grain basmati rice,
    soaked in cold water for 20
    minutes

Preheat the oven to 400°F.

Remove the skin and fat from the chicken. Cut the chicken into 8–10 serving pieces. Boil the wings, neck, and giblets in 1 cup of the water to make 1 cup of stock. In a blender or spice grinder, grind the pistachios, fennel, cumin, paprika, and garam-masala and whip them into the yogurt. Soak the saffron threads in the hot milk for 15 minutes.

Heat ¼ cup of the oil in a large saucepan. Add 1 of the onions and fry over medium heat until browned. Remove the onion and drain on paper towels. Add the almonds and raisins to the pan and fry until the almonds are golden brown and the raisins puffed. Add the cardamom, cinnamon, cloves, bay leaves, peppercorns, and nutmeg and fry, stirring occasionally, for 1–2 minutes. Add the remaining onion and the garlic and fry until browned. Mix in the pistachio paste and cook for 1–2 minutes, stirring constantly to prevent the sauce from sticking to the bottom of the pan. Add the chicken, salt, and strained stock and mix thoroughly. Cover and cook for 15 minutes, stirring once or twice. There should be a thick gravy with the half-cooked chicken. Mix in the fresh mint leaves.

Boil the rice in 2½ quarts of water and the remaining tablespoon of oil and cook over medium heat for 8 minutes until half done. Drain in a colander.

Transfer the chicken and gravy to a large casserole. Spread on the rice. Garnish with the almonds, browned onions, and raisins. Pour the saffron milk over the rice. Cover the dish tightly with aluminum foil and the lid. Bake for 15 minutes. Reduce the heat to 300°F and cook for another 15 minutes. Turn off the heat and leave the casserole in the oven for 5 minutes before serving. Serve on a platter with spinach, pappadams, and Cucumber, Onion, and Tomato Relish (see Index).

Shrimp Pilao Rice

(Jhinga Pilao)

Serves 6

2 pounds jumbo shrimps
1 teaspoon ground turmeric
¼ teaspoon ground dried red chilies
¼ cup vegetable oil
1 large onion, peeled and chopped fine
6 green cardamom pods
2 cinnamon sticks
¼ teaspoon whole cloves

½ teaspoon black peppercorns
3 bay leaves
Salt to taste
2 cups long-grain basmati rice, soaked in cold water for 20 minutes
½ cup canned cream of coconut
2 cups water
1 cup shelled fresh peas *or* 1 10-ounce package frozen peas

Preheat the oven to 400°F.

Shell and devein the shrimps. Transfer them to a large bowl and mix with the turmeric and ground chili; set aside.

Heat the oil in a large saucepan. Add the onion and fry over medium heat until browned. Remove the onion and drain on paper towels. Add the cardamom, cinnamon, cloves, peppercorns, and bay leaves to the pan and fry until the spices turn a shade darker. Mix in the shrimps and add the salt and stir thoroughly. Add the rice, cream of coconut, and water. Cover and simmer for 8–10 minutes, occasionally stirring gently to prevent the rice from sticking to the bottom of the pan. Turn off the heat. With a fork, stir in the peas. Cover, reduce the oven heat to 300°F, and bake for 7–10 minutes, until the liquid is absorbed. Garnish with browned onions and serve with vegetable sambar, pappadams, and coconut chutney.

Benares-Style Vegetable Pilao Rice

(Benaresi Sabzi Pilao)

Benares is famous for this fragrant, delicious vegetable pilao.

Serves 6

2 cups long-grain basmati rice	10 cloves
2½ quarts water	½ teaspoon black peppercorns
¼ cup vegetable oil	2 bay leaves
1 medium onion, peeled and chopped	1 medium head of cauliflower, cut into 1-inch flowerets
4 cloves garlic, peeled and crushed	1 cup shelled fresh peas *or* 1 10-ounce package frozen peas
1 ½-inch piece fresh gingerroot, peeled and grated	½ teaspoon ground turmeric
1 cinnamon stick	¼ teaspoon ground dried red chilies
8 green cardamom pods	Salt to taste

Wash the rice. In a large pot, boil the rice in the water with 1 tablespoon of the oil and salt over medium heat, stirring occasionally, for 5 minutes, until the rice is three-quarters cooked. Drain the rice in a colander and set aside.

Preheat the oven to 400°F.

Heat the oil (less 1 tablespoon) in a large saucepan. Add the onion, garlic, and ginger and fry over medium heat until browned. Add the cinnamon, cardamom, cloves, peppercorns, and bay leaves, stirring for 2 minutes. Add the cauliflower, peas, turmeric, ground dried red chilies, and salt, mixing thoroughly. Cover and simmer for 5 minutes.

Spread the cooked rice in a large casserole dish and stir in the cauliflower and peas gently. Cover the dish tightly with aluminum foil and the lid. Reduce the oven temperature to 300°F. Bake for 5–8 minutes. Turn off the heat and leave the casserole in the oven for 5 minutes. Serve hot with Sweet Mango Chutney (see Index), pappadams, and curry.

Vegetable Pilao Rice

(Sabzi ka Pilao)

Serves 6

2 cups long-grain basmati rice, soaked in cold water for 15 minutes

8¾ cups water

½ cup vegetable oil

Salt to taste

1 cup shelled fresh peas *or* 1 10-ounce package frozen peas

6 cloves garlic, peeled

1 1-inch piece fresh gingerroot, peeled and chopped

6 green cardamom pods, pods removed and discarded

2 fresh green chilies

6 cloves

1 cinnamon stick, broken into pieces

1 teaspoon ground turmeric

1 tablespoon poppy seeds

4 medium onions, peeled and sliced

¼ cup fresh mint leaves

1 teaspoon saffron threads

¼ cup hot milk

¼ cup blanched almonds

¼ cup raw cashews

¼ cup raisins

2 large carrots, peeled and cut into 1-inch pieces

2 large potatoes, peeled and cut into 1-inch cubes

1 small head of cauliflower, cut into small flowerets

1 large tomato, chopped

1 large green bell pepper, cut into rings

¼ cup chopped cilantro leaves

Wash the rice. In a large pot, boil the rice in 2 quarts of the water with 1 tablespoon of the oil and salt over medium heat, stirring occasionally, for 5 minutes, until the rice is three-quarters cooked. Drain the rice in a colander, mix the peas with the rice, and set aside.

Place ¼ cup of the water, the garlic, ginger, cardamom, green chilies, cloves, cinnamon, turmeric, poppy seeds, 3 of the onions, and the mint leaves in a blender and puree. Soak the saffron threads in the hot milk for 15 minutes.

Heat the oil (less 1 tablespoon) in a large saucepan. Add the remaining onion and fry over medium heat until browned but crisp. Remove the onion and drain on paper towels. Add the almonds, cashews, and raisins to the pan and fry until the nuts are light brown and the raisins have puffed. Remove and drain on paper towels. Add the pureed mixture to the pan and stir for 5–8 minutes, until the oil separates, stirring occasionally to prevent the mixture from sticking to the bottom of the pan. Stir in the vegetables (except the peas), the remaining ½ cup water, and salt, and mix thoroughly. Cover, reduce the heat, and cook for 5–7 minutes, until the vegetables are half done.

Preheat the oven to 400°F. Lightly grease a large casserole dish and place the vegetables in the dish. Garnish with cilantro leaves. Spread on the peas and rice in an even layer. Garnish the top of the rice with the browned onion, almonds, cashews, and raisins. Cover the dish tightly with aluminum foil and the lid. Place the dish in the oven, reduce the heat to 300°F, and bake for 7–10 minutes. Serve hot with legumes and Yogurt with Fresh Mint and Eggplant (see Index).

Easy Mixed Vegetable Pilao Rice

(Bhaji ka Pilao)

Serves 6

3 cups long-grain basmati rice, soaked in cold water for 20 minutes

¼ cup vegetable oil

1 teaspoon cumin seeds

2 bay leaves

1 cinnamon stick

4 black cardamom pods

½ teaspoon black peppercorns

¼ teaspoon whole cloves

3 large carrots, peeled and cut diagonally into 1-inch strips

1 pound green beans, cut diagonally into 1-inch strips

1 cup shelled fresh peas *or* 1 10-ounce package frozen peas

1 teaspoon ground turmeric

¼ teaspoon ground dried red chilies

Salt to taste

3½ cups water

Preheat the oven to 400°F. Wash the rice and drain it in a colander. Heat the oil in a large saucepan. Add the cumin seeds, bay leaves, cinnamon, cardamom, peppercorns, and cloves and fry over medium heat, stirring, for 8–10 seconds. Add the carrots, beans, peas, turmeric, ground chili, and salt and fry for 2–3 minutes. Add the rice and mix thoroughly for 2–3 minutes. Stir in the water, cover, and place in the oven. Reduce the heat to 300°F and bake for 10–12 minutes, until the rice and vegetables are done.

Serve hot with cilantro chutney, pappadams, and raita.

Basmati Pilao Rice

(Basmati Pilao)

Serves 6

2 cups long-grain basmati rice,
    soaked in cold water for 20
    minutes
6 green cardamom pods
¼ teaspoon whole cloves
3 bay leaves
1 cinnamon stick
½ teaspoon black peppercorns
1 medium onion, peeled and
    sliced fine
3 cloves garlic, peeled and sliced
    fine
1 tablespoon vegetable oil
1 quart water
Salt to taste

Preheat the oven to 400°F. Wash the rice and place it in a pot with all the other ingredients. Cover and cook over medium heat for 7–10 minutes, until rice is three-quarters cooked. Drain in a colander and transfer to a large casserole dish. Cover with aluminum foil and the lid. Place in the oven, reduce the heat to 300°F, and bake for 5–8 minutes. Turn off the heat and leave the casserole in the oven for 5 minutes before serving. Serve hot with your choice of curry, vegetables, and dal.

Rice with Lentils and Vegetables
(Masala Khichidi)

Serves 6

2 cups long-grain basmati rice
1 cup pink lentils
4 green cardamom pods, pods
 removed and discarded
6 cloves
1 cinnamon stick, broken into
 small pieces
1 tablespoon cumin seeds
¼ teaspoon black peppercorns
5¼ cups water
6 cloves garlic, peeled
1 1-inch piece fresh gingerroot,
 peeled and chopped

2 fresh green chilies
¼ cup vegetable oil
3 medium onions, peeled and
 sliced fine
¼ cup blanched almonds
¼ cup raisins
1 large potato, peeled and cut
 into ½-inch pieces
1 teaspoon ground turmeric
Salt to taste
½ coconut, shelled and grated
1 pound fresh mushrooms, sliced
¼ cup cilantro leaves

Soak the rice and lentils together in 1 quart of water for 20 minutes and drain in a colander. In a small skillet, roast the cardamom seeds, cloves, cinnamon, cumin, and peppercorns until the spices turn a shade darker. Place ¼ cup of the water, the garlic, ginger, green chilies, and roasted spices in a blender and puree.

Heat the oil in a large pot. Add 2 of the onions and fry over medium heat until browned. Remove the onions and drain on paper towels. Add the almonds and raisins to the pot and fry until the almonds are golden brown and the raisins are puffed. Remove and drain on paper towels. Add the remaining onion and the pureed mixture to the pot, stirring for 5 minutes, until the oil separates. Add the rice and lentils, potato, turmeric, salt, and grated coconut, mixing thoroughly for 5 minutes. Add the remaining 5 cups water and cook for 5–7 minutes, stirring occasionally to prevent the rice from sticking to the bottom of the pan. Add the mush-rooms and cilantro leaves and stir. Cover and cook for another 6–8 minutes, until the liquid has evaporated and the rice, lentils, and vegetables are done.

Serve hot, garnished with the browned onions, almonds, and raisins.

Spicy Madras-Style Lime Rice
(Puliharam)

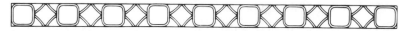

Serves 6

3 cups long-grain basmati rice,
    soaked in cold water for 20
    minutes
1½ quarts water
5 tablespoons vegetable oil
1 teaspoon ground turmeric
Salt to taste
1 tablespoon black mustard seeds
¼ teaspoon asafoetida powder
1 tablespoon split black beans
1 tablespoon yellow split peas
1 sprig curry leaves
5 fresh green chilies, chopped
Juice of 2 limes

Wash the rice and boil in the water with 1 tablespoon of the
oil, the turmeric, and salt over medium heat for 8–10 minutes, until the rice is done. Drain the rice in a colander and
return it to the pot. With a fork, gently separate the rice
grains. Preheat the oven to 350°F. Place the rice in the oven
to keep it hot.

Heat the remaining oil in a saucepan. Add the mustard seeds
and fry over medium heat. When the seeds start popping,
add the asafoetida and the beans and peas and fry until
golden brown. Add the curry leaves and green chilies, stirring for a few seconds. Remove from the heat and pour the
mixture over the rice. Squeeze the lime juice over the rice.
Serve hot with South Indian Madras–Style Legumes with
Vegetables (see Index), pappadams, and Fresh South Indian–Style Coconut Chutney (see Index).

◇ 12 ◇
Healthful Legume Dishes

Legumes in Garlic and Onions
(Dal)

Serves 6

2 cups pigeon peas, soaked in
cold water for 20 minutes
1 quart water
½ teaspoon ground turmeric
Salt to taste
¼ cup vegetable oil
1 tablespoon black mustard seeds
2 teaspoons cumin seeds
1 medium onion, peeled and
chopped fine
6 cloves garlic, peeled and
chopped fine
½ teaspoon ground dried red
chilies

Wash the pigeon peas and boil them in the water with the turmeric and salt over medium heat for 20 minutes, until the pigeon peas are done. Heat the oil in a medium sauce-pan. Add the mustard and cumin seeds and fry over medium heat until the mustard seeds start popping. Stir in the onion and garlic and fry until browned and soft. Mix in the ground chili and stir for 30 seconds. Remove and pour over the pigeon peas. Stir thoroughly, cover, and simmer for 10 minutes, stirring occasionally to prevent the pigeon peas from sticking to the bottom of the pot. Serve hot with plain rice, pappadams, and Goan Portuguese-Style Spicy Pork (see Index).

South Indian Madras-Style Legumes with Vegetables

(Madrasi Sambar)

Serves 6

1 cup pigeon peas or pink lentils, soaked in cold water for 15 minutes
1½ quarts water
1 teaspoon ground turmeric
Salt to taste
¼ cup vegetable oil
1 tablespoon black mustard seeds
¼ teaspoon fenugreek seeds
4 dried red chilies
1 medium onion, chopped and sliced fine
1 ½-inch piece fresh gingerroot, peeled and chopped fine
4 cloves garlic, peeled and crushed

1 tablespoon ground coriander
2 teaspoons ground cumin
¼ teaspoon freshly ground black pepper
⅛ teaspoon asafoetida powder
1 small eggplant, cut into 1-inch cubes
½ pound green beans, cut into 1-inch pieces
1 pound okra
2 large carrots, peeled and cut diagonally into 2-inch pieces
1 large tomato, chopped
2 teaspoons tamarind concentrate
¼ cup chopped cilantro leaves

Wash the pigeon peas and boil in the water with the turmeric and salt over medium heat for 15 minutes. Heat the oil in a saucepan. Add the mustard seeds, fenugreek seeds, and chilies and fry over medium heat until the mustard seeds start popping. Add the onion, ginger, and garlic and fry until the onion is golden brown. Stir in the coriander, cumin, pepper, and asafoetida and stir for 2 minutes, until the oil separates. Remove and mix in with the pigeon peas. Add the vegetables and the tamarind and stir. Cover and bring to a boil. Reduce the heat, cover, and simmer for 8–10 minutes, until vegetables are done, stirring occasionally to prevent the mixture from sticking to the bottom of the pot. Garnish with cilantro leaves and serve hot with plain rice, chutney, and pappadams or with a fish curry of your choice.

Zucchini Lentils
(Tori ka Dal)

Serves 6

1 pound pink lentils, soaked in
  cold water for 20 minutes
2 quarts water
½ teaspoon ground turmeric
¼ teaspoon ground dried red
  chilies
Salt to taste
¼ cup vegetable oil
½ teaspoon cumin seeds
2 medium onions, peeled and
  chopped fine
4 cloves garlic, peeled and
  chopped fine
1 ½-inch piece fresh gingerroot,
  peeled and chopped fine
1 large tomato, chopped
2 pounds zucchini, sliced into
  ¼-inch slices
1 tablespoon chopped cilantro
  leaves

Wash the lentils and boil them in the water with the turmeric, ground chili, and salt over medium heat for 15–20
minutes. Heat the oil in a medium saucepan. Add the cumin
seeds and fry until golden brown. Add the onions, garlic,
and ginger and fry until browned. Add the tomato and stir
until soft. Remove and mix with the lentils; cook over medium heat for 5–8 minutes. Mix in the zucchini and cook
for another 5 minutes. Garnish with cilantro leaves and
serve hot as a soup or with chapatis or plain rice and accompanying entrées.

Eggplant with Legumes

(Baigan ka Dal)

Serves 6

1 pound yellow split peas, soaked
 in cold water for 20 minutes
1½ quarts water
½ teaspoon ground turmeric
Salt to taste
¼ cup vegetable oil
1 teaspoon black mustard seeds
1 teaspoon cumin seeds
1 medium onion, peeled and
 chopped
5 cloves garlic, peeled and
 crushed
1 ½-inch piece fresh gingerroot,
 peeled and chopped fine
1 fresh green chili, chopped fine
1 tablespoon ground coriander
1 large tomato, chopped
1 large eggplant, cut into 2-inch
 cubes

Wash split peas and boil in the water with the turmeric and
salt over medium heat for 20 minutes. Heat the oil in a
saucepan. Add the mustard and cumin seeds and fry over
medium heat until the mustard seeds start popping. Add the
onion, garlic, ginger, and chili and fry until the onion is
browned and soft. Add the coriander and fry for 2 minutes,
stirring constantly. Add the tomato and cook for 3-5 minutes. Remove and stir into the split peas. Add the eggplant,
cover, and simmer for 8-10 minutes, until the eggplant is
done. Serve hot with plain rice or chapatis and Chicken
Curry (see Index), Yogurt with Spinach (see Index), and
pappadams.

Peshawar-Style Chick-Peas

(Peshawari Chana)

Serves 6

4 cups chick-peas, soaked in cold
  water overnight
1½ quarts water
Salt to taste
4 black cardamom pods
2 cinnamon sticks
6 cloves
¼ cup vegetable oil
1½ tablespoons ground cumin
½ teaspoon freshly ground black
  pepper
3 tablespoons ground coriander
2 teaspoons Basic Garam-Masala
  (see Index)
2½ tablespoons pomegranate
  seeds, washed
3 tablespoons mango powder
1 1-inch piece fresh gingerroot,
  peeled and chopped fine
2 fresh green chilies, chopped

Wash the chick-peas and boil in a large pot with the water,
the salt, cardamom, cinnamon, and cloves over medium heat
for 30 minutes, until the chick-peas are done. Heat the oil in
a small saucepan. Add the cumin, pepper, coriander, garam-
masala, and pomegranate seeds and fry over medium heat
for 2 minutes. Remove and stir into the cooked chick-peas
along with the mango powder, ginger, and green chilies.
Bring to a boil and remove from the heat. Garnish with
onions and wedges of lemon. Serve hot with chapatis or
plain rice.

Lucknow-Style Lentils

(Lucknawi Dal)

Serves 6

2 cups pink lentils, soaked in cold
  water for 20 minutes
1½ quarts water
Salt to taste
1 teaspoon ground turmeric
1 teaspoon tamarind concentrate
  or 1 tablespoon fresh lemon
  juice
¼ cup vegetable oil
1 tablespoon cumin seeds
1 large onion, peeled and
  chopped
6 cloves garlic, peeled and
  crushed
1 1-inch piece fresh gingerroot,
  peeled and chopped
½ teaspoon ground dried red
  chilies

Wash the lentils and boil them in the water with the salt,
turmeric, and tamarind (if you are using lemon juice, do not
add it now) over medium heat for 20 minutes, until the
lentils are done. Heat the oil in a small saucepan. Add the
cumin seeds and fry over medium heat for a minute. Stir in
the onion, garlic, and ginger and fry until the onion is
browned and soft. Add the ground chili and stir for 30
seconds. Remove and pour into the pot of lentils, mix thoroughly, and bring to a boil. If you are using lemon juice
instead of tamarind, add it before serving the lentils with
chapatis or plain rice, cauliflower, and lamb curry.

Legumes with Vegetables
(Dal aur Tamatar-Bhaji)

Serves 6

2 cups yellow split peas, soaked
   in cold water for 20 minutes
¼ cup vegetable oil
2 large onions, peeled and
   chopped
10 cloves garlic, peeled and
   chopped
1 1-inch piece fresh gingerroot,
   peeled and chopped
4 fresh green chilies, chopped
1 teaspoon ground turmeric
2 bunches (1 pound) fresh
   spinach, chopped coarse *or* 1
   10-ounce package frozen
   chopped spinach

3 large tomatoes, chopped
2 bunches (1 pound) mustard
   greens, chopped coarse *or* 1
   10-ounce package frozen
   mustard greens
1 medium eggplant, cut into
   1-inch cubes
1 large potato, peeled and cut
   into 1-inch cubes
½ cup chopped fresh dill
Salt to taste
1½ quarts water

Wash the split peas and set them aside. Heat the oil in a
large pot. Add the onions, garlic, ginger, and chilies and fry
over medium heat until the onions are golden brown. Add
the turmeric and stir for a minute. Add the split peas, vegetables, dill, and salt. Mix thoroughly for 5 minutes. Add the
water and bring to a boil. Reduce the heat, cover, and
simmer for 30–40 minutes, until the vegetables and split
peas are done, stirring occasionally to prevent the vegetables
from sticking to the bottom of the pan. Serve hot with
chapatis and plain rice, pappadams, hot mint chutney, and
beef curry.

South Indian Madras-Style Legumes
(Madrasi Rasam)

Serves 6

2 cups pigeon peas, soaked in
  cold water for 20 minutes
6½ cups water
¼ teaspoon ground turmeric
Salt to taste
1 teaspoon tamarind concentrate
1 tablespoon cumin seeds
½ teaspoon coriander seeds
¼ teaspoon fenugreek seeds
¼ teaspoon black peppercorns
2 dried red chilies

¼ cup vegetable oil
2 medium onions, peeled and
  sliced
5 cloves garlic, peeled and
  crushed
1 ½-inch piece fresh gingerroot,
  peeled and chopped fine
Pinch of asafoetida powder
3 sprigs curry leaves
1 large tomato, chopped

Wash the pigeon peas and boil in 1½ quarts of the water with the turmeric and salt over medium heat for 20 minutes until the peas are done. Keep them at a simmer. Soak the tamarind concentrate in the remaining ½ cup water for 10 minutes. In a small saucepan, roast the cumin, coriander, fenugreek, peppercorns, and chilies and grind to a fine paste. Heat the oil in a saucepan. Add the onions, garlic, and ginger and fry over medium heat until browned. Add the asafoetida powder and curry leaves and stir for 30 seconds. Stir in the ground spices, mixing thoroughly. Remove and add to the simmering pigeon peas. Add the tamarind water and the tomato and mix thoroughly. Bring the mixture to a boil and serve with plain rice, pappadams, and vegetables.

Rajeswari's South Indian Legumes with Vegetables

(Rajeswari ki Dakshini Sambar)

Serves 6

2 cups pigeon peas
9 cups water
½ teaspoon ground turmeric
Salt to taste
1 tablespoon tamarind
  concentrate
¼ cup plus 1½ teaspoons
  vegetable oil
1 tablespoon yellow split peas
1 tablespoon split black beans
4 dried red chilies
¼ teaspoon fenugreek seeds

¼ teaspoon asafoetida powder
1 large eggplant, cut into 1-inch
  cubes
1 pound green beans, cut into
  2-inch pieces
1 pound zucchini, cut into 1-inch
  slices
1 tablespoon black mustard seeds
3 sprigs curry leaves
¼ cup chopped cilantro leaves

Wash the pigeon peas and boil in 2 quarts of the water with the turmeric and salt over medium heat for 20 minutes until the peas are done. Keep them at a boil. Soak the tamarind concentrate in the remaining cup of water for 10 minutes.

Heat 1½ teaspoons of the oil in a small saucepan. Add the yellow split peas, split black beans, chilies, fenugreek seeds, and asafoetida and fry, stirring constantly, until golden brown. Put the mixture in a spice grinder and grind to a powder. Add the vegetables and tamarind water to the boiling pigeon peas. Cook for 5–8 minutes. Stir in the ground mixture, mix thoroughly, and cook for 5 minutes. Set aside.

Heat the remaining ¼ cup oil in a saucepan. Add the mustard seeds and fry over medium heat until they start popping. Add the curry leaves and stir for 15 seconds. Pour this over the pigeon peas and vegetables, mix thoroughly, add the cilantro leaves, and bring to a boil. Serve hot with plain rice, pappadams, and lamb curry.

Royal Legume Curry
(Shahi Dal)

Serves 6

2 cups pigeon peas, soaked in
cold water for 20 minutes
1½ quarts water
1 teaspoon ground turmeric
1 cinnamon stick
½ teaspoon black peppercorns
3 bay leaves
6 green cardamom pods
6 cloves
Salt to taste
¼ cup vegetable oil
1 medium onion, peeled and
sliced fine
1½-inch piece fresh gingerroot,
peeled and chopped fine
4 cloves garlic, peeled and sliced
fine
2 fresh green chilies, chopped
fine
1 large tomato, chopped

Wash the pigeon peas and boil them in the water with the turmeric, cinnamon, peppercorns, bay leaves, cardamom, cloves, and salt for 20 minutes, until the peas are done. Heat the oil in a saucepan. Add the onion, ginger, garlic, and green chilies and fry over medium heat until the onion is browned. Remove and pour over the pigeon peas, add the tomato, cover, and simmer for another 5–8 minutes, stirring occasionally to prevent the pigeon peas from sticking to the bottom of the pot. Serve hot with chapatis or pilao rice, Chicken Curry in Yogurt Mint Sauce (see Index), and Cucumber, Onion, and Tomato Relish (see Index).

Mulligatawny Beef Soup with Legumes
(Moloogu-Thanee Dal-Gosht)

You can substitute 2 pounds of chicken, skinned and cut into ½-inch pieces, for the beef if you wish.

Serves 6

1 cup split mung beans, soaked in cold water for 20 minutes

2 pounds lean beef stew meat, cut into ¼-inch cubes

Salt to taste

½ teaspoon ground turmeric

½ teaspoon ground dried red chilies

½ teaspoon black peppercorns

2 cinnamon sticks

3 bay leaves *or* 2 sprigs curry leaves

2 quarts water

1 large onion, peeled and chopped

6 cloves garlic, peeled and chopped

1 1-inch piece fresh gingerroot, peeled and chopped fine

2 teaspoons ground cumin

1 tablespoon ground coriander

1 tablespoon Basic Curry Powder (see Index)

¼ cup vegetable oil

1 tablespoon black mustard seeds

¼ teaspoon fenugreek seeds

1 large potato, peeled and cut into ½-inch cubes

3 large carrots, peeled and cut into 1-inch pieces

2 tomatoes, chopped

Wash the beans and place in a large pot with the meat, salt, turmeric, ground chili, peppercorns, cinnamon, bay leaves, and water. Boil over medium heat for 15–20 minutes until the meat and beans are tender.

Place the onion, garlic, ginger, cumin, coriander, and curry powder in a blender and puree. Heat the oil in a saucepan. Add the mustard and fenugreek seeds and fry over medium heat until the mustard seeds start popping. Stir in the pureed mixture and fry for 5–8 minutes, until the oil separates. Remove and add to the meat and peas. Cover and cook for 10 minutes, stirring occasionally. Add the potato, carrots, and tomato and cook for 8–10 minutes, stirring occasionally, until done. Remove cinnamon sticks, bay leaves, and peppercorns before serving. If desired, you can also add 1 cup of cooked rice.

Mulligatawny Soup
(Moloogu-Thanee)

Serves 4

½ cup yellow split peas soaked in
   cold water for 20 minutes
1 pound lean beef stew meat, cut
   into ¼-inch cubes
1 pound beef bones
Salt to taste
2 quarts water
1 tablespoon coriander seeds
2 teaspoons cumin seeds
¼ teaspoon fenugreek seeds
1 tablespoon black mustard seeds
4 cloves garlic, peeled
12 black peppercorns
5 curry leaves

In a pot, mix the peas, meat, bones, salt, and water. In a small skillet, roast all the remaining ingredients except the curry leaves. Add the roasted spices to the pot and boil over medium heat 30–45 minutes, until the meat and peas are done. Mix in the curry leaves and cook for another 5 minutes. Remove the bones and strain the whole spices and seeds. Serve hot with the meat in soup bowls.

◇ 13 ◇
Wholesome Breads

Deep-Fried Unleavened Puffy Bread

(Poori)

Serves 6 (12 pooris)

2 cups whole-wheat flour
1 cup all-purpose unbleached
    flour
Salt to taste
3 cups plus 2 tablespoons
    vegetable oil

1 cup warm water, warm milk, or
    buttermilk
½ cup whole-wheat flour for
    dusting

In a large bowl, mix the flours, salt, 2 tablespoons of the oil, and the water until a dough is formed. Place the dough on a clean cutting board or other surface dusted with a little flour. Knead the dough for 10 minutes, until smooth. Cover with a damp cheesecloth and leave at room temperature for 15–20 minutes.

Divide the dough into 12 equal parts and roll into smooth balls. Coat each ball with flour and flatten to form a patty. Set the patty on a clean cutting board or other surface and with a rolling pin make a 5- to 6-inch round tortilla or flat cake, lightly dusting the dough with wheat flour to prevent it from sticking to the rolling pin and cutting board.

Heat the remaining 3 cups oil in a wok over high heat. When the oil is hot gently drop 1 flat bread into the hot oil. The bread will sink to the bottom. Hold a steel spatula over the bread for 2–4 seconds to help it cook. Gently press the bread for another 2–4 seconds to help it puff up. Once the bread starts to puff up, cook for 10–15 seconds and turn the bread over; cook for another 10–15 seconds. Remove and drain the bread on paper towels. Repeat this process until all the bread is cooked.

Serve immediately with any vegetarian fare or your favorite curry.

Nutritious Whole-Wheat Baked Bread
(Chapati)

Serves 6 (12 chapatis)

3 cups whole-wheat flour
Salt to taste
1 cup warm water, warm milk, or
  buttermilk
½ cup whole-wheat flour for
  dusting
1 tablespoon vegetable oil

In a medium bowl, mix the flour and salt with the water until a dough is formed. Place the dough on a clean cutting board or other surface dusted with a little wheat flour, add the oil, and knead the dough for 10 minutes, until smooth. Cover with a damp cheesecloth and leave at room temperature for 15–20 minutes.

Divide the dough into 12 equal parts and roll into smooth balls. Coat each ball with flour and flatten to form a patty. Set the patty on a clean cutting board or other surface and with a rolling pin make a 5- to 6-inch round tortilla or flat cake, lightly dusting the dough with wheat flour to prevent it from sticking to the rolling pin and cutting board.

Heat an iron griddle over high heat and then reduce the heat to medium. Gently lift 1 flat bread and place it on the hot griddle. Bake for 20–30 seconds, until the top of the chapati starts to puff a little. With tongs, turn the chapati over and bake for another 30–40 seconds, until the surface of the bread starts to puff. Remove and place on a clean napkin or covered dish. Repeat this procedure until all the chapatis are baked. Serve immediately.

Whole-Wheat Flaky Bread
(Paratha)

Serves 6 (12 parathas)

2 cups whole-wheat flour
1 cup all-purpose unbleached
  flour
1 teaspoon carom seeds
Salt to taste

1 cup warm water, warm milk, or
  buttermilk
½ cup vegetable oil
½ cup whole-wheat flour for
  dusting

In a large bowl, mix the flours, carom seeds, salt, water, and 1 tablespoon of the oil until a dough is formed. Place the dough on a clean cutting board or other surface dusted with a little wheat flour and knead the dough for 10 minutes, until smooth. Cover with a damp cheesecloth and leave at room temperature for 15–20 minutes.

Divide the dough into 12 equal parts and roll into smooth balls. Coat each ball with flour and flatten to form a patty. Set the patty on a clean cutting board or other surface and with a rolling pin make a 5- to 6-inch round tortilla or flat cake, lightly dusting the dough with wheat flour to prevent it from sticking to the rolling pin and cutting board.

Heat an iron griddle over medium heat. Brush each bread with ⅛ teaspoon of the oil and fold the bread in half; again brush a little oil on the bread and fold it again to make a triangle. Dust with wheat flour, flatten, and with a rolling pin roll out a 6-inch triangle, dusting with flour to prevent the bread from sticking to the rolling pin and cutting board.

Pour ¼ teaspoon of the oil on the griddle and gently place the bread on the hot griddle. Fry for a minute, until the bread starts to puff up a little. With tongs, turn the bread over, brush on ½ teaspoon oil, and cook for a minute. Move the bread around on the griddle without flipping it and cook evenly for 30–40 seconds. Remove and cover to keep warm. Repeat this process until all the bread is fried.

Serve hot with spinach beef or yogurt chicken and chutney.

Garlic Wheat Bread

(Lahsun ka Paratha)

Serves 4 (8 parathas)

2 cups whole-wheat flour
5 cloves garlic, peeled and crushed
1 teaspoon carom seeds
Salt to taste

½ cup vegetable oil
1 cup warm water or milk
¼ cup whole-wheat flour for dusting

In a large bowl, mix the flour, garlic, carom seeds, salt, 1 tablespoon of the oil, and the water until a dough is formed. Knead the dough for 7–10 minutes, until smooth. Cover with cheesecloth or a cloth napkin and set aside for 20 minutes.

Divide the dough into eight equal portions. Roll each portion into a smooth ball and roll out with a rolling pin to a 7-inch tortilla or flat cake, occasionally dusting with wheat flour to prevent sticking. Heat an iron griddle over medium heat. Brush the griddle with 1 teaspoon of the oil and gently place the bread on the hot griddle. Fry for 2–3 minutes, until golden brown and crisp. Turn over and brush 1 teaspoon oil over the bread and griddle. Fry for 2–3 minutes, until golden brown and crisp. Remove, cover, and keep warm. Repeat this process until all the bread is fried.

Serve hot with Chicken Curry in Cashew Sauce (see Index), legumes, and Sweet Mango Chutney (see Index).

Oven-Baked Leavened Bread
(Nan)

Serves 8 (8 nans)

2 tablespoons fresh compressed
   yeast *or* 1 ¼-ounce envelope
   active dry yeast
½ cup warm milk
2 tablespoons sugar
½ cup plain low-fat yogurt
1 large egg, beaten lightly
3 tablespoons vegetable oil, plus
   extra for brushing
Salt to taste
4 cups all-purpose unbleached
   flour
¼ cup warm water if needed
¼ cup all-purpose unbleached
   flour for dusting if needed
1 tablespoon black onion seeds

In a small bowl, dissolve the yeast in ¼ cup of the warm milk. Stir in 1 teaspoon of the sugar and let it sit in a warm place for 10 minutes, until the mixture begins to froth. (This is to test if the yeast is alive. If it does not froth, begin the test with a fresh batch of yeast until mixture froths.)

Lightly whip the yogurt and add the remaining sugar and milk, the egg, 3 tablespoons oil, and salt. Stir in the yeast mixture. Place the flour in a large bowl and pour in the yogurt mixture. Mix thoroughly to form a large ball of dough. Knead for 10–15 minutes, until the dough is smooth, using the additional water if necessary, dusting occasionally with a little flour if the dough begins to stick. Cover the dough with cheesecloth or a cloth napkin and set aside for 4 hours, until the dough has doubled in size.

Preheat the oven to 500°F.

Punch down the dough and knead it for 1–2 minutes, until smooth. Divide it into eight equal portions. Roll each portion into a smooth ball and use a rolling pin to flatten the ball out to a 7- to 8-inch oval tortilla or flat cake. Brush with a little oil and sprinkle the black onion seeds over the bread. Spread on two shallow baking pans or ungreased cookie sheets and place in the center of the oven. Bake for 3 minutes, until the bread has puffed and turned golden brown. Remove and wrap in a clean napkin to keep warm. Repeat this process until all the bread is baked.

Serve hot with your choice of vegetables and curry entrée or Roast Chicken Marinated in Yogurt and Lemon Masala (see Index).

Whole-Wheat Bread Stuffed with Potato
(Alu ka Paratha)

Serves 4 (8 parathas)

Stuffing

4 medium potatoes, peeled,
  boiled, and mashed
2 tablespoons finely chopped
  cilantro leaves
½ teaspoon roasted Basic Garam-
  Masala (see Index)
¼ teaspoon ground dried red
  chilies
Juice of ½ lemon
Salt to taste

Bread

2 cups whole-wheat flour
Salt to taste
¾ cup warm water or milk
½ cup whole-wheat flour for
  dusting
¼ cup vegetable oil

Prepare the stuffing: Mix all of the stuffing ingredients and divide into eight equal portions.

Prepare the bread: In a large bowl, mix the flour, salt, and water until a dough is formed. Place the dough on a clean cutting board or other surface dusted with a little wheat flour and knead the dough for 10 minutes, until smooth. Cover with a damp cheesecloth and leave at room temperature for 15–20 minutes.

Divide the dough into eight equal portions. Roll each into a smooth ball and make a deep indentation in the center. Fill with potato stuffing and then cover the filling evenly with dough. Gently flatten each ball to a patty. With a rolling pin, gently roll the patties out to smooth 6-inch round tortillas or flat cakes, occasionally dusting with wheat flour to prevent the dough and stuffing from sticking to the rolling pin and cutting board.

Heat an iron griddle over medium heat and brush with 1 teaspoon of the oil. Gently place 1 bread on the hot griddle and cook for a minute, until golden brown. Turn over and brush the bread with 1 teaspoon oil. Cook for another minute, until the bread is golden brown and crisp. Repeat this process until all the bread is cooked.

Serve hot with legumes, Chicken Curry in Yogurt Mint Sauce (see Index), and Sweet Mango Chutney (see Index).

Whole-Wheat Bread Stuffed with Carrots
(Gajar ki Roti)

Serves 4 (8 roti)

Bread

2 cups whole-wheat flour
Salt to taste
1 cup warm water or milk
½ cup vegetable oil
¼ cup whole-wheat flour for
  dusting

Filling

3 tablespoons vegetable oil
½ teaspoon black mustard seeds
1 small onion, peeled and
  chopped fine
2 cloves garlic, peeled and
  crushed
1 ¼-inch piece gingerroot, peeled
  and chopped fine
1 fresh green chili, chopped fine
2 large carrots, peeled and grated
  fine
Salt to taste

Prepare the bread: In a large bowl, mix the flour, salt, water, and 1 tablespoon of the oil until a dough forms. Knead for 7–10 minutes, until smooth. Cover with a cheesecloth or cloth napkin and set aside for 20 minutes.

Prepare the filling: Heat the oil in a medium skillet. Add the mustard seeds and fry over medium heat until they start to pop. Add the onion, garlic, ginger, and green chili and fry until the onion is browned and soft. Stir in the carrots and salt and cook for 5 minutes, until the liquid has evaporated. Remove and set aside.

Fry the bread: Knead the dough for a minute and divide it into eight equal portions. Roll each portion into a smooth ball and roll out with a rolling pin to a 5-inch tortilla or flat cake. Spread 1 tablespoon of the carrot mixture evenly over the bread, fold the dough in half, and brush with oil. Fold the dough in half again to make a triangle and dust with flour. Roll out with a rolling pin to make a 6- to 7-inch flat triangle.

Heat an iron griddle over medium heat and brush with 1 teaspoon oil. When the oil is hot, gently place 1 bread on the griddle and fry for 2 minutes, until golden brown and crisp. Turn the bread over and brush with 1 teaspoon oil. Fry for 1 minute, until golden brown and crisp. Remove, cover, and keep warm. Repeat this process until all the bread is fried.

Serve hot with Muslim-Style Fragrant and Spicy Beef Meatballs (see Index), Hot Cilantro Relish (see Index), and legumes of your choice.

Bread Stuffed with Ground Meat and Mint Leaves

(Pudina Kheema ki Roti)

Serves 4 (8 roti)

Filling

2 tablespoons vegetable oil
1 small onion, peeled and
    chopped fine
2 cloves garlic, peeled and
    chopped fine
1 ¼-inch piece fresh gingerroot,
    peeled and chopped fine
½ teaspoon Basic Garam-Masala
    (see Index)
½ pound lean ground lamb, beef,
    or turkey
Salt to taste
1 tablespoon finely chopped fresh
    mint leaves

Bread

1 cup all-purpose unbleached
    flour
1 cup whole-wheat flour
1 cup warm water or milk
½ cup vegetable oil
Salt to taste
¼ cup whole-wheat flour for
    dusting

Prepare the filling: Heat the oil in a small saucepan. Add the
onion, garlic, and ginger and fry over medium heat until

browned. Stir in the garam-masala and fry for 40-50 seconds. Add the meat, salt, and mint leaves and fry for 3-4 minutes, until the meat is browned evenly. Cover, reduce the heat, and simmer for 5-7 minutes, until the meat is done. Remove and set aside.

Prepare the bread: In a large bowl, mix the flours, water, 1 tablespoon of the oil, and the salt until a dough is formed. Knead the dough for 7-10 minutes, until smooth. Cover with cheesecloth or a cloth napkin and set aside for 20 minutes.

Knead the dough for a minute and divide it into eight equal portions. Roll each portion into a ball and roll out with a rolling pin to a 5-inch tortilla or flat cake. Spread 1 tablespoon of the filling evenly on the bread and fold the bread in half. Brush with oil and fold in half again to make a triangle. Gently roll out with a rolling pin to a 6- to 7-inch flat triangle, dusting with wheat flour to prevent sticking.

Heat an iron griddle over medium heat and brush with 1 teaspoon of the oil. When the oil is hot, gently place 1 bread on the griddle, and fry for 3-4 minutes, until golden brown and crisp. Turn over and brush 1 teaspoon oil over the bread. Fry for 2 minutes, until golden brown and crisp. Remove, cover, and keep warm. Repeat this process until all the bread is fried.

Serve hot with Yogurt with Potato, Cucumber, and Cilantro (see Index) and Eggplant with Legumes (see Index).

Whole-Wheat Bread Stuffed with Mozzarella Cheese and Spicy Chicken
(Azami Paratha)

Serves 4 (8 parathas)

Bread

2 cups whole-wheat flour
Salt to taste
1 cup warm water or milk
½ cup vegetable oil
¼ cup whole-wheat flour for
    dusting

Stuffing

1 large whole chicken breast, skin
    and bones removed
1 cup water
Salt to taste
3 tablespoons vegetable oil
1 small onion, peeled and
    chopped fine
3 cloves garlic, peeled and grated
1 ¼-inch piece gingerroot, peeled
    and chopped fine
1 fresh green chili, chopped fine
½ teaspoon ground coriander
¼ teaspoon ground cumin
½ cup grated mozzarella cheese

Prepare the bread: In a large bowl, mix the flour, salt, water, and 1 tablespoon of the oil until a dough forms. Knead for 7–10 minutes, until smooth. Cover with a cheesecloth or cloth napkin and set aside for 20 minutes.

Prepare the stuffing: Chop the chicken into small pieces. Boil the chicken in the water with the salt over medium heat for 15 minutes, until cooked. With a sharp knife, chop the chicken into very fine pieces and set aside. Heat the oil in a small saucepan. Add the onion, garlic, ginger, and green chili and fry over medium heat until the onion is browned. Stir in the coriander and cumin and fry for 1 minute. Add the chicken pieces and fry for 2–3 minutes, stirring and mixing thoroughly. Remove and set aside.

Fry the bread: Knead the dough for a minute and divide it into eight equal portions. Roll each portion into a smooth ball and roll out with a rolling pin to a 6-inch tortilla or flat cake. Spread 1 tablespoon of the chicken mixture over the bread. Cover the chicken with 1 tablespoon mozzarella. Fold the bread in half. Brush with oil and fold in half again to make a triangle. Dust with wheat flour and gently roll out with a rolling pin to make a 6- to 7-inch flat triangle.

Heat an iron griddle over medium heat and brush with 1 teaspoon of the oil. When the oil is hot, gently place 1 bread on the griddle and fry for 2–3 minutes, until golden brown and crisp. Turn over and brush with 1 teaspoon oil. Fry for 2–3 minutes, until golden brown and crisp. Remove, cover, and keep warm. Repeat this process until all the bread is fried.

Serve hot with Sweet Mint Chutney (see Index) and legumes.

Bread Stuffed with Spinach
(Sag ka Paratha)

Serves 6 (12 parathas)

2 bunches (1 pound) fresh
  spinach, chopped, cooked,
  drained, and mashed with a
  fork
2 fresh green chilies, chopped
  fine
2 cups whole-wheat flour
1 cup warm milk or water
¾ cup vegetable oil
Salt to taste
¼ cup whole-wheat flour for
  dusting

Thoroughly mix the spinach and chilies. In a large bowl,
mix the flour, water, 1 tablespoon of the oil, and the salt
until a dough is formed. Knead for 5–8 minutes, until the
dough is smooth. Divide the dough into 12 balls. With a
rolling pin, roll out each ball to a flat 5-inch pancake.
Spread 1 tablespoon of spinach paste evenly over the bread
and fold the bread in half and then in half again to make a
triangle. Brush lightly with oil and gently roll out with a
rolling pin to a 6-inch triangle, occasionally dusting with
wheat flour to prevent sticking.

Heat an iron griddle over medium heat and brush with 1
teaspoon of the oil. Gently place the bread on the hot griddle and fry for 2 minutes, until golden brown and crisp.
Turn over and brush on 1 teaspoon oil. Fry for another
minute, until golden brown and crisp. Remove, cover, and
keep warm. Repeat this process until all the bread is fried.

Serve hot with Spicy Chicken Roast (see Index) and legumes.

◇ 14 ◇
Seductive Desserts

Semolina Halwa
(Suji ka Halwa)

Serves 6

½ cup milk
1 cup water
¾ cup sugar
½ teaspoon saffron threads
½ cup margarine or vegetable oil
1 cup fine semolina
¼ cup raisins or sultanas
¼ cup slivered blanched almonds
1 teaspoon ground green
    cardamom

In a medium saucepan, boil the milk, water, sugar, and
saffron threads over medium heat, stirring constantly for 5–
7 minutes, until the sugar dissolves. Remove from the heat
and set aside. Heat the margarine in a large saucepan. Add
the semolina and fry over medium heat, stirring for 8–10
minutes, until golden brown. Pour in the sugar syrup, raisins, almonds, and ground cardamom, stirring constantly
for 8–10 minutes until the pudding thickens and the liquid
is absorbed. Remove and pour evenly into a lightly greased
medium-size platter. Cool and cut into serving pieces. Serve
warm or cold.

Carrot Halwa

(Gajar ka Halwa)

Serves 8-10

3 quarts milk
2 cups light brown sugar
3 pounds carrots
¼ pound (½ cup) margarine
  or ¼ cup vegetable oil
½ cup slivered blanched
  almonds

½ cup chopped unsalted pistachios
¾ cup milk fudge
½ cup plus 2 tablespoons honey or
  light brown sugar
2 teaspoons crushed green
  cardamom seeds

Prepare the milk fudge: Place 2 quarts of the milk and the brown sugar in a large pot. Boil over medium heat for 15–20 minutes, until the milk cooks down to one-quarter the original volume, stirring constantly to prevent the milk from sticking to the bottom of the pot. Lower the heat and simmer for 1 hour and 15 minutes, stirring constantly, until the milk becomes a thick creamy fudge. Remove from heat, transfer to a lightly greased bowl, and set aside to cool.

Peel and grate the carrots. Set aside in a large bowl. Heat the margarine in a large saucepan. Add the almonds and pistachios and fry over medium heat until golden brown. Stir in the carrots. Cover and cook for 10–12 minutes, until the carrots are tender. Add the milk fudge and the remaining quart of milk and cook for 20–30 minutes, stirring occasionally, until the milk is absorbed and the halwa is moist (it should not be dry). Add the honey and cardamom and stir until the sugar has dissolved and the carrots appear glazed and sticky. Cook for 2–3 minutes, stirring constantly. The halwa should be thick. Remove, pour into a lightly greased platter, cool, and cut into 2-inch squares. Serve hot or cold. Carrot halwa can be stored in the refrigerator for 3–4 days.

Coconut Fudge
(Nariyal ki Barfi)

Serves 10

1 cup milk
2 tablespoons margarine or
vegetable oil
2 cups sugar

1 coconut, shelled and grated
1 teaspoon ground green
cardamom

Lightly grease a medium-size shallow baking pan or cookie sheet. In a large saucepan, bring the milk and margarine to a boil over medium heat. Stir in the sugar and add the grated coconut and cardamom, stirring constantly for 6–8 minutes, until the coconut becomes thick and glazed. Remove from the heat and pour into the baking pan. Cool, cut into squares, and serve.

Cashew Fudge
(Kaju ki Barfi)

Serves 10

2 cups unsalted raw cashews
1 quart milk
1 cup light brown sugar
¼ teaspoon ground green
cardamom

1 tablespoon margarine or
vegetable oil

Soak the cashews in a bowl of boiling water for about an hour. Drain in a colander. Place 1 cup of the milk and the cashews in a blender and puree. Lightly grease a medium-size shallow baking pan or cookie sheet.

In a pot, heat the remaining 3 cups milk, the sugar, cardamom, and margarine over medium heat for about 15 minutes, stirring constantly, until the sugar dissolves and the mixture is thick. Add the cashew paste and mix thoroughly to prevent the cashews from sticking to the bottom of the pan. Cook and stir for 4–6 minutes, until the nut paste is thick and sticky. Remove from the heat and spread evenly in the baking pan. Cool, cut into squares, and serve.

Almond Fudge

(Badam ki Barfi)

You can substitute unsalted raw pistachios or walnuts for the almonds in this recipe.

Serves 10

2 cups blanched almonds
1 quart milk
1 cup sugar
¼ teaspoon ground green
  cardamom

1 tablespoon margarine or
  vegetable oil

Place the almonds and 1 cup of the milk in a blender and puree. In a saucepan, heat the remaining 3 cups milk, the sugar, and cardamom over medium heat for 8–10 minutes, stirring constantly, until the sugar dissolves and the mixture is thick. Add the almond paste and the margarine, mix thoroughly, and cook for 15–20 minutes, until the fudge is thick and smooth. Remove from the heat and spread evenly in the baking pan. Cool, cut into squares, and serve.

Carrot Pudding

(Gajar ki Kheer)

Serves 8

½ teaspoon saffron threads
4¼ cups milk
3 pounds carrots
1 cup sugar
¼ teaspoon ground green
   cardamom
¼ cup slivered blanched almonds
2 tablespoons margarine or
   vegetable oil

Soak the saffron threads in ¼ cup hot milk.

Peel and grate the carrots. In a large saucepan, boil the remaining quart of milk, sugar, cardamom, almonds, and margarine over medium heat for 5–6 minutes, stirring occasionally. Add the grated carrots and mix thoroughly, cooking for 15–20 minutes, until the mixture thickens and the carrots are glazed and sticky. Pour the saffron milk over the mixture and stir for 1–2 minutes. Remove from the heat and serve warm or cold.

Sweet Vermicelli Pudding

(Seviyan)

Serves 6–8

1 cup fine vermicelli
½ teaspoon saffron threads
2¼ cups milk
¼ cup margarine or vegetable oil
¾ cup sugar
¼ cup slivered blanched almonds
¼ cup raisins or sultanas
½ teaspoon ground green
cardamom

Break the vermicelli into 1- to 2-inch pieces to make stirring easy. Soak the saffron threads in ¼ cup hot milk for 15 minutes.

Heat the margarine in a saucepan. Add the vermicelli and fry over medium heat for 4–5 minutes until golden brown, stirring as the color changes. Add the milk and bring to a boil, stirring occasionally. Add the saffron milk and stir. Cover, reduce the heat, and simmer gently for 7–8 minutes, until the vermicelli is tender, stirring occasionally to prevent the ingredients from sticking to the bottom of the pan. Add the sugar, almonds, raisins, and cardamom and stir thoroughly for a minute. Remove from the heat and serve warm or chilled in dessert bowls.

Rice Pudding
(Kheer)

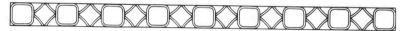

Serves 6

½ cup long-grain basmati rice
2 cups water
2 quarts milk
5 green cardamom pods
1¼ cups sugar
¼ cup slivered blanched almonds
½ teaspoon ground cardamom
¼ teaspoon ground nutmeg
1 tablespoon rose water

Wash the rice and boil in the water over medium heat for 5–6 minutes, until the rice is one-quarter done. Drain in a colander.

In a saucepan, bring the milk and whole cardamom pods to a boil over medium heat. Add the rice and cook for 30–40 minutes, until the rice is soft and the milk very thick. Stir occasionally at first and then constantly when the milk begins to thicken, to prevent the ingredients from sticking to the bottom of the pan. Add the sugar, almonds, ground cardamom, and nutmeg and cook for another 5 minutes, stirring constantly.

Remove from the heat and set aside. Remove the cardamom pods from the pudding and sprinkle with the rose water. Serve warm or chilled in dessert bowls.

Sweet South Indian Milk Dessert
(Payasam)

Serves 8

1 cup sago (tapioca)
2 cups water
3 tablespoons margarine or
  vegetable oil
¼ cup finely chopped blanched
  almonds
¼ cup finely chopped unsalted
  blanched pistachios
2 teaspoons crushed green
  cardamom seeds
1½ quarts milk
1 cup sugar
½ cup vermicelli, broken into 2-
  inch pieces
½ cup shredded coconut
¼ cup raisins or sultanas

In a bowl, soak the sago in the water for an hour. Heat the margarine in a saucepan. Add the almonds and pistachios and sauté over medium heat until golden brown. Remove the nuts and drain on paper towels. Add the cardamom to the pan and stir for 20 seconds. Pour in the milk and sugar and bring to a boil. Reduce the heat and simmer for 10 minutes, stirring constantly, until the sugar dissolves. Drain the sago and add it to the milk. Cook for another 5 minutes, stirring constantly. Stir in the vermicelli and mix thoroughly for 3–4 minutes. Add the coconut, raisins, almonds, and pistachios and simmer for 5 minutes, stirring constantly to prevent the ingredients from sticking to the bottom of the pan. Remove and pour into dessert bowls. Chill before serving.

Cream Cheese Patties in Pistachio and Cardamom Sauce

(Rasa Malai)

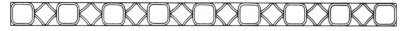

Serves 10

Cream Sauce

2 quarts milk
4 cups sugar

Cheese Patties

2 quarts milk
¼ cup fresh lemon juice
1 tablespoon all-purpose
   unbleached flour
⅛ teaspoon baking powder

Syrup

2 quarts milk
1 cinnamon stick
1 tablespoon crushed green
   cardamom seeds
4 cups sugar

Garnish

¼ cup finely slivered blanched
   almonds
¼ cup finely chopped unsalted
   blanched pistachios

Prepare the cream sauce: In a pot, boil the milk and sugar over medium heat for 15-20 minutes, stirring constantly. Reduce the heat to low and simmer for 1 hour, stirring constantly with a steel spatula until the milk is reduced to a little less than 2 cups and is a thick, creamy sauce. Remove and set aside to cool.

Prepare the cheese patties: In a pot, boil the milk over medium heat for 5 minutes. Reduce the heat and add the lemon juice, stirring constantly for 10–15 seconds, until the milk curdles and separates from the whey, which will be a yellowish color. Remove and drain in a cheesecloth tied to the faucet over the sink until all the liquid has drained—1 to 1½ hours. Remove the cheese and set it on a clean cutting board or other surface. Knead for 5–6 minutes, until the cheese is the consistency of dough. Add the flour and baking powder and knead thoroughly to make a soft and smooth dough. Divide the dough into 16 equal portions. Roll into smooth balls and flatten lightly to the thickness of a cookie; set aside.

Prepare the syrup: Place the milk, cinnamon stick, and crushed cardamom in a pot and bring to a boil; boil for 10 minutes. Stir in the sugar and cook over medium heat until dissolved. Reduce the heat and simmer for 5 minutes.

Cook the cheese patties: Gently place the cheese patties in the simmering milk syrup, cover, and cook for 20–25 minutes. The cheese patties should puff up and float on the surface of the syrup. Turn off the heat and cool. Discard the cinnamon stick. Refrigerate until you are ready to serve.

Assemble the dessert: Gently and carefully remove the cheese patties from the milk syrup and place them on a dessert platter. Pour the milk syrup evenly over the patties. Garnish with almonds. Pour the cream sauce evenly over the almonds and cheese patties. Sprinkle with chopped pistachios. Cover and refrigerate for at least 2–3 hours before serving.

◇ 15 ◇
Traditional Beverages

○

There is a famous legend that Daruma, the Indian Buddhist monk and founder of Zen Buddhism, once fell asleep while meditating. In a fit of anger at his weakness, he tore off his eyelids and tossed them away. Where the eyelids fell there sprang a bush, the leaves of which had the magic property of banishing fatigue and malaise. Thus was born the divine beverage called tea.

For more than two centuries the three famous teas of India—Darjeeling, Assam, and Nilgiris—have stirred the hearts, stimulated the minds, and soothed the palates of mankind. Even in countries that grow their own teas today, India tea remains the favorite.

India and Sri Lanka (Ceylon) are the largest producers of fine teas in the world. In India, as in Sri Lanka, black Darjeeling teas are cultivated under snowcapped mountains. These teas are known for their exquisite flavor and distinctive aroma. Black Assam tea is grown at the foothills of the Himalayas and is strong, pungent, and full-bodied. The famous Lipton teas come from India and Sri Lanka. The teas of Nilgiris (Blue Hills in South India) are of a bright, brisk quality with distinct flavors.

As with wine, black tea is made by crushing and fermenting the delicate raw materials. The leaves are "withered" first, then spread on wire racks and warmed for 24 hours. Soon the leaves become limp and can be "rolled" by hand or by machine. The rolling breaks up the cells in the leaves and releases the natural juices and enzymes, which are the keys to the flavor of the tea. The freshly rolled leaves are spread on immaculate tables in a cool, humid environment for proper fermentation. It is a three-hour process and turns the leaves a copper color.

Perhaps the most critical time is knowing just when to choke off the oxidation by "firing" or heating, and it is accomplished by carefully controlled driers. Drying the leaves in hot-air chambers stops the fermentation, and the leaves turn dark brown or black.

Sifting machines vibrate the leaves into various grades. There are two basic categories: whole leaf and broken leaf. Leaf size is not an indication of tea quality any more than the color of a grape determines how fine a wine it will make. Like fine wine, tea must be tasted for its quality to be judged.

Indian Spiced Tea
(Masalewali Chai)

The people in the cooler regions of India have traditionally added spices to their tea, not just for flavoring but also to induce heat in the body. Spiced teas are particularly welcome after a satisfying Indian meal. This recipe is richly accented with cardamom, cloves, and cinnamon.

Serves 6

7 cups cold water
1 cup milk
1 cinnamon stick
6 green cardamom pods
6 cloves
1 ¼-inch piece fresh gingerroot, peeled and chopped
¼ cup light brown sugar or honey
2 tablespoons Darjeeling, Assam, or Nilgiris tea

In a pot, bring the water and milk to a boil over medium heat. Stir in the spices and brown sugar. Boil for 5 minutes and turn off the heat. Cover the pot and let the spices steep for 10 minutes. Add the tea leaves and bring the water to a boil. Cover, reduce the heat, and simmer for 5 minutes. Strain the tea and serve immediately.

Cardamom Tea
(Elaichi Chai)

Serves 6

7 cups water
12 green cardamom pods
2 tablespoons Darjeeling or
    Assam tea
1 cup milk
¼ cup light brown sugar or honey

In a pot, bring the water and cardamom to a boil over medium heat and boil for 5 minutes. Remove the pot from the heat and set aside for 5 minutes. Add the tea leaves, bring to a boil, and boil for 2–3 minutes. Add the milk and brown sugar. Remove from the heat, strain the tea, and serve immediately.

Hot and Spicy Himalayan Tea

(Garam Himalaya Chai)

A hot cup of aromatic Darjeeling tea flavored with spices completes a sumptuous Indian meal.

Serves 6

1 tablespoon fennel seeds or
    aniseeds
6 green cardamom pods
12 cloves
1 cinnamon stick
1 ¼-inch piece fresh gingerroot,
    peeled and chopped
½ teaspoon black peppercorns
2 bay leaves
6 tablespoons light brown sugar
    or honey
7 cups water
2 tablespoons Darjeeling tea
1 cup milk

Place all ingredients except the tea and milk in a pot. Cover and boil over medium heat for 20 minutes. Remove from the heat, add the tea leaves, and set aside for 10 minutes. Add the milk and bring to a boil. Strain the tea into teacups and serve hot with dessert.

Refreshing Sandalwood Drink

(Sandal ka Sharbat)

Serves 6

1½ quarts water
5 cloves
5 green cardamom pods
½ teaspoon saffron threads
4 drops sandal essence, 1 ounce
 sandalwood, or 4 teaspoons
 sandalwood water
1 cup light brown sugar or honey
Juice of 1 lemon
1 cup plain low-fat yogurt
1 quart tonic water or plain soda
 water

Put the water, cloves, cardamom, saffron threads, and sandalwood in a pot and boil over medium heat for 5–6 minutes. Add the brown sugar and boil until dissolved and the syrup becomes thick. Remove and set aside. Add the lemon juice, stir, and cool.

Place the yogurt and cooled syrup in a blender and puree for a minute, until the liquid turns frothy. Pour into a bowl, mix with the tonic or soda water, and serve cold in medium glasses with ice cubes.

Yogurt Drink

(Lhassi)

Serves 6

1 quart plain low-fat yogurt
2 tablespoons rose water *or* 4
   drops of rose essence

6 tablespoons light brown sugar
   or honey
6 ice cubes

Place the yogurt, rose water, and brown sugar in a blender and puree. Add the ice cubes and blend for a minute, until the yogurt is whipped. Serve in tall glasses.

Mango-Yogurt Drink

(Aam ka Lhassi)

Serves 6

3 ripe mangoes
3 cups plain low-fat yogurt *or* 1
   quart buttermilk
3 tablespoons light brown sugar
   or honey
6 ice cubes

Peel the mangoes, remove the pulp from the seed, and transfer it to a blender with the yogurt and brown sugar. Blend for 30 seconds, until the mixture is whipped and creamy. Add the ice cubes and blend for 10 seconds. Remove and serve in wineglasses.

Fresh Papaya-Yogurt Drink
(Papita ka Lhassi)

Serves 6

1 medium-size ripe papaya
3 cups plain low-fat yogurt *or* 1
  quart buttermilk

3 tablespoons light brown sugar
  or honey
6 ice cubes

Peel and chop the papaya. Place the yogurt, papaya, and
brown sugar in a blender and blend for 1–2 minutes, until
pureed. Add the ice cubes and blend for 10 seconds. Remove
and serve in wineglasses.

Almond-Pistachio Milk
(Badam-Piste ka Sharbat)

Serves 6

1½ quarts milk
½ teaspoon saffron threads
6 tablespoons honey
¼ cup slivered blanched almonds
¼ cup chopped unsalted blanched
  pistachios

½ teaspoon crushed green
  cardamom seeds
¼ teaspoon crushed cloves
4 drops rose essence or 2
  tablespoons rose water
6 ice cubes

Place the milk, saffron threads, honey, almonds, pistachios,
cardamom, cloves, and rose essence in a pot and boil over

medium heat for 20–30 minutes. Remove from heat and set aside to cool. Transfer the mixture to a blender along with the ice cubes. Blend for 1–2 minutes, until the milk appears whipped and creamy. Serve in wineglasses.

Saffron-Almond Milk
(Z'affran Badam ka Sharbat)

Serves 6

1 teaspoon saffron threads
¼ cup hot milk
½ cup slivered blanched almonds
1½ quarts milk
½ teaspoon crushed green
   cardamom seeds
6 tablespoons light brown sugar
   or honey
6 ice cubes

Soak the saffron threads in the hot milk for 15 minutes. Place the almonds, milk, saffron milk, cardamom, and brown sugar in a blender and blend for 1–2 minutes, until whipped. Add the ice cubes and blend for 20–30 seconds. Serve in wineglasses.

◇ 16 ◇

The Sun, Moon, Stars, and Your Body

For more than 5,000 years the Hindu society has employed astrologers to master one of the oldest sciences known to mankind—the study of the sun, moon, and stars in relation to ourselves and our bodies. The Hindu zodiac analyzes actual events and circumstances destined to occur by virtue of one's karma, or past actions, speech, and thought. The Hindus believe that each person's present suffering and enjoyment are traceable directly to his or her previous karma and that we reap sorrow, disappointment, and pain when we have sown folly, made errors, or caused pain to another human being at some time in the past—if not in this life, then in some former birth. A horoscope prepared by an expert astrologer is an extraordinary blueprint for living that is concerned with propitiousness (timeliness) and the most elusive quality in life—truth.

Today nothing compares with Hindu astrology in terms of accuracy in predicting actual events and circumstances in one's life. When my sisters, brother, and I were born, the family astrologer was present at the hospital, preparing our horoscopes, calculating mathematical progressions according to the planetary positions and patterns (the physical arrangement of the planets in a chart), and interpreting them in relation to each other based on the date, place, and time of our birth.

I have, since the age of five, been fascinated by the sun, moon, and stars and have carefully followed their paths in relation to events in my life and the lives of those close to me. When I was growing up in Lucknow, our resident astrologer, Punditji, a tall, thin-faced ascetic figure with brilliant deep-set eyes, would make his appearance religiously every Sunday morning at 10:00 in our home, his Sanskrit charts and calendars clutched under his left arm. After his tea he would spread out his charts and calendars on the table on the veranda and would proceed to brief my mother on the following week's planetary patterns, activities, and disturbances and their effects on my parents' household. I can also vividly remember him advising my mother on the foods, herbs, and spices we should take for the maintenance of our good health.

Over the years the science of astrology has helped make life—and dealing with its realities, opportunities, and pitfalls—a little easier for me. For some people facing reality is generally a painful and distasteful task. Astrology gives us the basic elements to prepare for future events and meet life's problems as challenges. How we can overcome these obstacles is the true measure of how successful we really are.

As human beings we all seek, to the best of our ability, to attain a balanced existence in a world full of disharmony and imbalances. The motions of the heavenly bodies exert a profound influence on every aspect of our lives, including what we eat. You must remember that your health can always be improved, and planetary afflictions can be largely changed or overcome through self-discipline, proper diet, regular exercise, and harmonious thoughts. This is the view long held by both Hindu and Western astrologers, who maintain that the natives of each of the 12 signs of the zodiac have certain nutritional requirements and deficiencies that are intrinsic to their planetary type.

Proper diet alone, however, does not ensure freedom from illness. Emotions play an important role in the manifestation of our physical ailments. We know only a part of our being, our superficial intellect. There is a great deal more beneath that surface that we know nothing about, although it has its effects on our behavior. What happens in our lives depends on whether we react positively or negatively to the energies present. Tension is nothing more than stored energy, which can be used constructively or destructively.

I have therefore written this chapter specifically to help you understand your body, both physically and spiritually, and to develop your awareness of health and nutrition. Included in the following pages are a basic analysis of personality components, common physical afflictions, and dietary needs of each of the 12 zodiac signs.

 *Aries (Mesha Rasi)*

You are an Aries (Ram), the first sign of the zodiac, if you were born between March 21 and April 19. You are ruled by the planet Mars. Some astrologers believe Pluto to be your other planetary ruler. Your complementary or opposite sign is Libra.

You are a cardinal (initiating) fire sign, which, combined with your ruling planet's Martian energy, makes you a vital and dynamic personality. You are a leader, stimulated by danger, striving to be "first" at all times. You enjoy starting new projects, and you burst forth quickly into action and passion. You are often headstrong and enthusiastic. Like the other two fire signs, Leo and Sagittarius, you are most expressive, bold, intense, and adventurous. You seek to impress others, and you need to be admired for your singularity of purpose. You are usually quick and active, and your overabundance of energy makes it very difficult for you to slow down. You represent pure intuition, and you have a good brain, but you are inclined to act first and think later. In other words, you are impetuous.

Your courage is legendary, and serious physical disabilities are bravely met. You rarely suffer from the types of ill health that are caused by psychological difficulties, as you do not fret over things and relationships. You are, however, often prone to accidents because of your quick and hasty movements. You should exercise great caution in handling sharp tools or instruments and in driving an automobile. You tend literally to rush into things (not looking where you are going) and to overestimate your physical power to cope with all the demands that your active brain puts on you. Burns, bruises, and cuts are part of being an Aries native. It is imperative that you make a concerted and conscious effort to slow down to reduce accidents and help you be more relaxed. You desperately need some of the "balance" of your opposite and complementary sign, Libra. If you wish to remain in perfect health, you should make sure you get mental as well as physical relaxation. Any physical exercise that calls for coordination of body and mind is most suitable for you. Deep-breathing yoga exercises alleviate tension and anger and certainly will help you relax.

Apart from accidents, you may also be susceptible to headaches and migraine; dental problems; eye, nose, and ear infections; feverish conditions and vertigo; nervous exhaustion; and head colds. Many, if not all, of these conditions can prevented by paying careful attention to your daily habits, self-discipline, and a well-balanced diet. You will also probably react positively to acupuncture and massage therapy.

Aries rules the head in general, specifically the motor centers of the brain and the circulation of the blood through the skull region. Therefore, the most active part of your body is your brain. Generally speaking, you should guard against head colds and eye strains and should have frequent dental checkups. Proper diet will go a long way toward maintaining a balance in your bodily functions.

For you, psychological and spiritual health is described as "balance"; your need to project yourself is obsessive and usually takes up all your energy. You are an extrovert, and although your brain may be very active, you never stop for a minute to think where your haste is taking you. Because of the tensions that this sort of life creates, illness may strike unexpectedly.

You should avoid quarrels or mental stress, often brought on by your quick temper and resentment of all criticism, justified or not. Sometimes you are not very tactful in communicating with others. In your hurry to get things done, you are inclined to be a little callous, insensitive, or inconsiderate. You must learn to recognize the rights and the worth of other people. At times you can be stubborn and refuse to listen to reason. If things do not go your way, some of you are apt to become nervous or irritable and sometimes even destructive.

As for your diet, you need to eat foods such as rhubarb, broccoli, carrots, potatoes, peas, dairy products, honey, nuts, seafood, sunflower and sesame seeds, tomatoes, radishes, onions, mustard, cauliflower, lettuce, watercress, spinach, beets (raw), lemons, grapefruit, cucumbers, dates, grapes, apples, walnuts, and celery. Your diet should also include an adequate amount of organic iron and muscle-building proteins, found in lean meat and legumes. Some of the common herbs associated with your sign are garlic, mustard, chamomile, rosemary, aloe, basil, capsicum, capers, oregano, red pepper, peppermint, and horseradish. Your body needs foods containing potassium phosphate, present in a wide variety of green vegetables and potatoes, onions, apples, and walnuts. The vitamins and minerals you need are A, B_1, B_2, B_6, D, P, choline, inositol, niacin, manganese, potassium, and zinc.

- You should cultivate patience, tolerance, sympathy, and moderation.

- You should avoid dissipation of your life force (energy), obstinacy, and alcohol.
- Companions harmonious with your sign are Leo, Sagittarius, Libra, Cancer, and Capricorn.

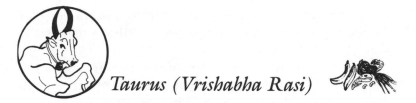

Taurus (Vrishabha Rasi)

You are a Taurus (Bull) if you were born between April 20 and May 20. Like Libra, Venus is your ruling planet. Your opposite or complementary sign is Scorpio. Yours is a fixed sign, which means you evaluate and endure to form something of tangible value. You do not like making changes. You are staunch, stalwart, upright, trusting, and honorable. You are also cautious, dependable, stable, reliable, and loving.

You are a peace-loving and nonviolent creature unless you are provoked—then you will attack, regardless of the size or strength of your adversary. You are tenacious—indeed your obstinacy is well known and could work against you—and are known for your ability to concentrate. Once your mind is made up, you seldom change it. This, in fact, is the most outstanding feature of your character. Whatever you attempt to do, you pursue with great determination and industry, and you invariably complete what you start. Generally you achieve what you want through your ability to persevere. You are thorough and do not believe in shortcuts. Your patience and painstaking efforts invariably pay off in the long run, and you learn to rely on yourself. You dislike being told what to do and you do not like being contradicted. Some of you Taurus natives may have a tendency to be cautious and suspicious of others. Sometimes you find it difficult to forget or forgive.

You have very little trouble getting along with people; it is your nature to be helpful to anyone in need. You are also tolerant and warm. You enjoy peace and harmony and crave it in your home life. Where affairs of the heart are concerned, you are capable of great tenderness and affection. You are intensely loyal to friends. You are also extremely sensitive to psychic currents and emotional influences around you.

You have a tremendous need to feel secure and to have both feet firmly on the earth under you. You are a nature lover. You are practical, sensitive, and creative as an artist. The influence of your ruling planet, Venus, endows you with a melodious voice and gives you an appreciation for beauty in all of the arts. You are a connoisseur of the finer things of life. You value material possessions and creature comforts. Sensory gratification is important to you, and you can be very sensual.

Taurus rules the adenoids, tonsils, larynx, and thyroid glands. The most common health problems you are likely to have during your lifetime are throat infections; diseases involving the larynx, neck, ears, and sex glands; diphtheria; asthma; sinusitis; and disabilities stemming from overindulgence in rich foods. Getting adequate physical exercise is vital to you if you want to avoid circulatory problems, which haunt Taurus natives who lead inactive lives. You should cultivate walking, yoga exercises, playing golf, swimming, and dancing. You enjoy massages. Your attitude toward illness tends to be gloomy, and this combined with your stubbornness in not adhering to your doctor's orders may mean prolonging your sickness. You have a negative and pessimistic attitude toward health, and you prefer putting up with ill health to treating yourself or finding a cure.

Many of your health problems can be prevented or corrected by proper diet. Your natural fondness for starchy foods, sweets, and pastries may give you an early start toward being overweight, a tendency that may be irreversible in middle age. Try to eat less. You have a strong constitution, and many of you remain extremely healthy. Since you have a deep-seated fear of disease and are very susceptible to negative suggestions regarding your health, you should cultivate a more optimistic outlook, bearing in mind that natives of your sign usually exhibit a formidable resistance to most diseases. You can benefit from a natural diet and need to curb your love of rich food and good wine. Educate your fine palate to appreciate wholesome foods.

You should eat seafood, chard, cabbage, onions, beets, pumpkin, leeks, raspberries, beans, almonds, bananas, avocados, grapes, apples, and all the foods containing sulfate of soda and iodine. Herbs most commonly associated with your sign are sage, comfrey, nutmeg, and wintergreen. The vitamins and minerals you need are A, B_{15}, E, F, iodine, phosphorus, zinc, selenium, magnesium, and manganese.

- You should cultivate optimism and flexibility and deep-breathing yoga exercises to relax.
- You should avoid anger, brooding, excessive stubbornness, uncontrolled emotion, procrastination, self-indulgence, and exhaustion of your personal resources.
- Companions harmonious with your sign are Leo, Scorpio, Aquarius, Capricorn, and Virgo.

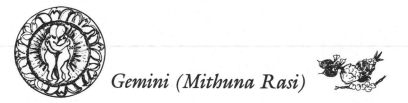

Gemini (Mithuna Rasi)

You are a Gemini (Twins) if you were born between May 21 and June 21. Mercury is your ruling planet. You are a mutable air sign, which means you are versatile, sensitive, intelligent, nervous, and very curious about life. Your opposite and complementary sign is Sagittarius.

You are charming, quick-witted, curious, often fickle, and pleasure-loving. You can overpower one with warm affection one instant and suddenly change into an emotional iceberg the next. Your character is as changeable as quicksilver. You have a highly developed mind and imagination.

You are nervous, and you talk a lot. You have the talent to amuse and elevate the spirits of most people.

Your agile mind and motion suggest that you are intelligent and have a tendency to attempt too much; therefore you suffer from nervous exhaustion. This means strict discipline on your part is necessary to get any of your projects completed. Since you are an air type, you are concerned with all matters of communication. Literature and art are alluring to you. Creativity in almost any form fascinates you.

As you are a cerebral or thinking type rather than a feeling or emotional type, you seldom form deep and permanent friendships. In fact you do not become attached to any place or thing either—much less to your ideas. On an emotional level you tend to conceal deep feelings. Like the other air signs, Libra and Aquarius, you get very distressed, and perhaps it is for this very reason you tend to remain distant and detached. Your world is motion and activity, where beliefs and ideas change as swiftly as new communication is received. You are talented translators of all energy and can carry out tasks initiated by others. Your bipolar intellect gives you the capacity to consider two or more points of view simultaneously. You can be inclined to deceive yourself.

You abhor being tied down to drudgery, routine, or monotony. Your greatest enemy is boredom. You are threatened by restrictive conditions and can suffer from psychosomatic illnesses caused by boredom. It is vital for you to have a career that keeps your mind active. Although you find it very difficult to relax, it is imperative for your well-being to find ways to do so.

You must find the time to stop and listen to your inner self. You need to cultivate close relationships and to express your feelings. Your perpetual pursuit of things sometimes leaves you little time for people. Your superficial relationships leave you feeling not only lonely and dissipated but also disagreeable and disenchanted. To avoid this tendency, you should spend some of your time in reflection, contemplation, and the cultivation of deeper relationships.

Gemini rules the hands, arms and shoulders, chest, lungs, bronchi, and nervous system. Thus your body is susceptible in the areas of arms, shoulders, lungs, bronchial tubes, the nervous system, and the brain. You need a lot of sunshine, air, and outdoor exercise to relax both your body and your mind. Deep-breathing yoga exercises are one of the best forms of relaxation for you; they quiet the mind, and the exercises are slow and controlled.

You can be careless about your health because some of you tend to be "fast-food junkies." Your daily diet should include foods that restore exhausted nerves, increase vim and vigor, and regulate fibrin. This means a protein diet that includes lean meat, seafood, eggs, cheese, nuts, and soybeans. Your diet should also be balanced to include vegetables and fruits. Calcium foods are also especially important to you because they help calm jumpy nerves. Yogurt, milk, turnips, beans, and kale are common sources of this mineral. Vitamin D is needed to aid absorption of calcium. You also need to eat lettuce, cauliflower, carrots, garlic, parsley, celery, raspberries, strawberries, okra, licorice, corn, apricots, peaches, and plums. Herbs most commonly associated with your sign are comfrey, nutmeg, chives, ginger, rosemary, thyme, red clover, and hops. The vitamins and minerals you need are A, B_1, B_8, B_{12}, B_{15}, E, H (biotin), calcium, lecithin, niacin, selenium, zinc, and magnesium.

- You should cultivate deeper relationships, tranquillity, self-discipline, goal-directed action, pragmatism, and thoroughness.
- You should avoid nervous exhaustion, scattering your energies and spreading yourself too thin, inconstancy, which works against you, and repressing and suppressing your feelings.
- Companions harmonious with your sign are Virgo, Libra, Sagittarius, Aquarius, and Pisces.

Cancer (Kataka Rasi)

You are a Cancer (Crab) if you were born between June 22 and July 20. The moon is your ruling "planet." Your moods are very sensitive to the various phases of the moon. The moon's influence over your health is felt more acutely in infancy and childhood than in your mature years. You are a cardinal water sign, which means creation, ambition, activity, tremendous stress and remarkable achievement, and a desire for immediate recognition. Your opposite and complementary sign is Capricorn.

You are intuitive, sensitive, timid, empathetic, tender, shy, kind, patient, imaginative, domestic, pleasure-loving, capricious, frugal, loving, and sympathetic. You are maternal and protective and like to take care of everyone in your family. Your family is everything to you, and you are constantly worrying about family members. As a matter of fact, you are the worriers of the zodiac. Nothing can be more upsetting to you than unhappy conditions in your home. If you feel that your loved ones do not care or have neglected you, you will sulk and possibly suffer digestive troubles as an adult. You are usually loyal and faithful, highly sensitive to the moods of others, and will defend the underdog.

You have a deep need for acceptance, recognition, and approval. You tend to make rather unreasonable and heavy demands on those close to you and others and require constant reassuring. Left to your own devices, you can very easily become a dreamer, building castles in the air. But when impelled to action by the harsher realities of life, you are capable of great fortitude. You are more easily hurt than you care to show; and you have a tendency to dwell in the past, brooding over past slights and hurts. This is true of all water signs, but particularly of Cancer natives. You should understand that this fixation on the past is, of course, a sheer waste of time and energy and injures no one but yourself. Highly sensitive when your feelings are hurt, you will crawl right into your shell, like the crab, to nurse your wounds. Some of you find it difficult to enjoy yourself in environments outside your home. Sometimes you find it painful to face life, and you quietly resign yourself to being a fatalist.

When you are happy, you have a healthy sense of humor, and usually your health is good during such times. You attract illness when you become negative, gloomy, and pessimistic, setting up a vicious chain. The typical Cancer native rarely finds the private world of his or her own making a satisfactory one. The result is inner conflict and unfounded suspicions, which are manifested in physical maladies such as nervous indigestion, ulcers, gastritis, stomach disorders, and poor elimination, all of which are brought on by tension. Because of personal disappointments, hurts, and worries, you may at times be tempted to indulge in mind-altering drugs and alcohol. Be careful, because such overindulgences ultimately cause ill health and emotional disturbances.

In true maternal fashion, you are usually good homemakers and take immense pride in being great cooks. The trouble is, you have an appetite for good food and an inclination to overindulge; you find rich pastries, ice cream, and other sweets rather irresistible. You should try to control this tendency to overeat, which is especially strong when you are under some kind of mental or emotional stress. Most of you begin to put on weight fairly early in life, a predisposition that often leads to an imbalance in the essential metabolism of the body, as well as to edema. Since dancing often appeals to you, you should cultivate it as a regular form of exercise to "fight the flab." Walking in the open air and by the water, meditating, and doing deep-breathing yoga exercises will also do wonders for your mental, physical, and emotional well-being. Most of you need body massage to help eliminate fluid and to break down fatty tissue. Natural foods, especially the fibrous material such as bran and whole fruits (including the skins of apples and pears, etc.) are valuable to your health. Your worrying nature and sense of self-preservation can turn you into a hypochondriac. The only way to combat this tendency is to keep yourself busy.

Your basic diet should lean heavily toward proteins and should include a certain amount of seafood to ensure adequate intake of iodine. In addition, you require a variety of fruits, vegetables, and leafy greens. You should try to avoid consuming too many dairy products. Your body needs red cabbage, pumpkin, onions, oranges, lemons, egg yolks, watercress, seafood, spinach, tangerines, kale, raisins, papaya, raspberries, strawberries, yogurt, and rye bread. Herbs helpful for you are watercress, rosemary, sage, peppermint, chamomile, fennel, fenugreek, licorice, alfalfa, nutmeg, horseradish, parsley, arrowroot, caraway, cloves, mustard, thyme, chives, and vanilla. The vitamins and minerals you need are A, B_1, B_2, B complex, C, D, E, K, calcium, selenium, zinc, folic acid, chlorine, cobalt, niacin, lecithin, magnesium, manganese, molybdenum, phosphorus, and sulfur.

- You should cultivate self-confidence and emotional balance, trust, optimism and cheerfulness, and a spirit of forgiveness.
- You should avoid moodiness, overdosing on milk products, a self-pitying attitude and bitterness, suspicion, worry and apprehension, holding grudges, and overeating.
- Companions harmonious with your sign are Scorpio, Pisces, Libra, Capricorn, and Aries.

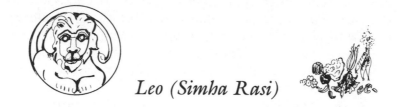

Leo (Simha Rasi)

You are a Leo (Lion) if you were born between July 21 and August 21. The sun is your planetary ruler. You are a fixed fire sign, which means you express yourself intuitively, often dramatically, in some enterprising manner. Most of you have sunny dispositions since the sun is your natural planetary ruler. Your opposite and complementary sign is Aquarius.

You are forceful, commanding, forthright, ambitious, fond of pleasures, affectionate, gentle, loyal, romantic, astute, generous, good-natured, and extremely kind. You are reliable and honorable, even though your obstinacy is well known. You are endowed with tremendous physical energy and resilient powers. Your whole life is represented by dynamic intensity of purpose and action. You must create and grow, turning your potential into reality. The terms *creation*, *recreation*, and *procreation* describe the various ways in which you can express yourself. You are earnest in expressing total joy in living. You are a doer and a go-getter and often end up in a position of power in the business world, where you have a tendency to exhaust yourself. You are too proud to ask for help from other people, and you often find yourself in situations where the pressure is more than you can bear. You are direct in almost everything you do and mean what you say. You have a quick mind and can make a decision in a very short time. You are not superficial or glib. There is nothing small or petty about you. You are particularly good with children.

Your arrogance and conceit are your downfall. You can be quite high-handed. Your opinion of yourself is often far too high, and some of you can be quite materialistic. Egocentric and insufferable, some of you are callous about what others think or feel. You realize, of course, that all of this is nothing more than a veneer or a cover-up for an inferiority complex, perhaps something that stems from an overly repressive childhood. You can be quite domineering and rather overbearing, and if this can be avoided there is no doubt that you are probably the kindest sign of the zodiac. In fact your overgenerosity can be a problem at times.

Psychologically you need to learn to appreciate the virtues of other people and the value of money. Sometimes you are lazy and procrastinate, and some of you can be compulsive gamblers.

The principal diseases of your sign are ailments related to the heart and to its function. You can also experience brief illnesses brought on by high fever or be plagued with back pains and spinal troubles. You are not usually subject to chronic, lingering maladies but to acute disorders that strike suddenly and are of short duration. Your fervent zest in both work and play adds to diseases resulting from pleasures, amusements, love affairs, and passionate excesses. Moderation is very good for you. Sleep is essential to you, as prolonged loss of sleep can seriously injure your ability to work efficiently or safely.

You should have a nutritional program that is high in protein and low in sugar and starches. You must avoid overweight, stress, and an improper diet. Foods you need to eat are peas, prunes, honey, cheese, spinach, cauliflower, citrus fruits, eggs, seafood, lettuce, blueberries, and nuts. Your body's need for vitamin E can be met if you include in your daily diet wheat germ, lettuce, and vegetable oils (especially soybean oil). Foods that supply adequate protein and help correct poor circulation include lean meats, game, fowl, yogurt, cheese, eggs, and beans. Helpful herbs for you are cayenne, garlic, rose hips, mustard, rosemary, dill, fennel, parsley, mint, and dandelion. The vitamins and minerals you need are B_1, B_{12}, C, E, F, H (biotin), choline, calcium, lecithin, magnesium, phosphorus, vanadium, and zinc. The vitamins most important to your sign are C and E. Natural vitamin C is supplied by citrus fruits, tomatoes, rose hips, watercress, cantaloupe, and strawberries.

- You should cultivate tact, deliberation, and tolerance.
- You should avoid arrogance, anger, conceit, haste, and excitement.
- Companions harmonious with your sign are Scorpio, Sagittarius, Aquarius, Aries, and Taurus.

 *Virgo (Kanya Rasi)*

You are a Virgo (Virgin) if you were born between August 22 and September 22. Your ruling planet is Mercury. Your opposite and complementary sign is Pisces. You are a mutable earth sign, which means you are versatile, sensitive, intelligent, nervous, and deeply curious about life.

You possess a penetrating and attentive mind and are imaginative, and you think a lot. You are studious and quick to learn. Your ability to use your critical faculties is well developed, and your accuracy sometimes amazes others. You are observant and sensitive to how others feel and can see below the surface of a situation. You are also interested in communication, and you talk a lot. You are generally plain spoken and down-to-earth. You have no trouble expressing yourself. You are well informed and have a keen interest in the arts and literature.

Your inner desire for order and efficiency manifests itself in tidiness and personal neatness. You are practical and not afraid of hard work, and you are a good planner. You try to do everything to perfection. You really cannot put up with delay or disorder. You can work patiently sorting out the most minute details, and you can get very impatient when any delay occurs. Most of the time you blame others when things do not go your way. Nothing is ever quite right for you, especially if someone else has done the work. You set very high goals both for yourself and for others, and you are never quite satisfied with what is accomplished. You have a tendency to run yourself ragged through the immense effort you put into every insignificant detail.

You are the opposite of Leo, who has the vast vision and the ability to organize on a grand scale; you are interested in the tiny details. Unlike most Leos, you tend to adhere to a temperate way of life, avoiding excesses. Your instinct for value is strong, and it is related to thought and judgment rather than to possessions.

You are profoundly analytical, reserved, and cautious and find it inconceivable to experience love in the passionate sense, because total self-surrender is an aversion to you. Yet, at the same time, your heart flows with human kindness. You take an intellectual approach to marriage, which your mate may find hard to comprehend, and you should choose your mate carefully, for lack of domestic harmony can lead to illness.

You cannot bear to have anything at all go wrong with you, and you have an intrinsic fear of disease. Therefore you have an extraordinary interest in matters concerning health, diet, and hygiene. As a matter of fact, your curiosity in these matters can easily become almost an obsession. In addition, you have a tendency to brood over the vaguest symptoms and even imagine yourself ill. Because of your negative attitude, your doctor could find it hard to restore you to health. It is of utmost importance for you to think of the well-being of your body rather than project yourself as an indiscriminate latent victim of maladies and illnesses, whether imaginary or real. You must have positive thoughts and turn your mind away from disease, not toward it. To improve your health you must learn to develop an inner sense of detachment to match the exterior mask of reticence that you often put on.

You are liable to suffer from digestive troubles, hypoglycemia, diarrhea, peritonitis, colitis, and hernia. These problems can be overcome by a healthy mental attitude and lifestyle. Natural foods and whole grains are good for you. Your delicate digestive system and your well-being can be at stake if you do not exercise caution in your eating habits.

Foods you need to eat are protein foods, endive, almonds, chicory, carrots, salad vegetables, whole wheat and rye, oats, lemons, peaches, prunes, parsley, cheese, yogurt, spinach, summer squash, zucchini, celery, okra, citrus fruits, plums, apples, dates, walnuts, and oranges. Herbs helpful to you are fennel, nutmeg, linseed, cloves, dill, fenugreek, sage, caraway, and summer savory. The vitamins and minerals you need are A, B complex, B_1, B_2, B_8, B_{12}, B_{15}, E, C, H (biotin), P, calcium, folic acid, inositol, lecithin, niacin, chlorine, magnesium, manganese, molybdenum, phosphorus, potassium, and sulfur.

- You should cultivate an expansive outlook, warmth, a greater variety of interests, and sympathy for your fellow workers.
- You should avoid enslaving yourself to "serve" others, being hypercritical and judgmental, becoming involved with trivia, and paying excessive attention to nonessential details.
- Companions harmonious with your sign are Sagittarius, Capricorn, Pisces, Taurus, and Gemini.

Libra (Tula Rasi)

You are a Libra (Scales) if you were born between September 23 and October 22. Venus is your planetary ruler. Your complementary and opposite sign is Aries. You are a cardinal air sign, which means creation, ambition, activity, tremendous stress and remarkable achievement, and a desire for immediate recognition.

You are an extrovert and concerned with personal relationships. Your desire to find a mate with whom you can communicate is very strong. You are kind and considerate and help those in need. You are charming, loyal, and good-natured. You seem to have no trouble getting along with most people as you are well liked and socially much in demand. You are gentle, somewhat withdrawn, and subtle in affairs of the heart.

Many of you are artistically inclined, for yours is a sign associated with art and beauty. Like the Taurus native, who is also ruled by Venus, goddess of love and beauty, you appreciate all the good things of life. Some of you can be very materialistic as you enjoy possessions and luxuries. You can also be vain and a trifle jealous. You are proud to entertain your guests in your home. For you it is important to dine in pleasing surroundings and with cheerful table companions.

Your obsessive need to balance everything can be a hindrance to you, and your conflict arises when the scales do not balance; as a result your health suffers. You are so good at seeing both sides of a situation that very often you cannot arrive at a decision. This vacillating affects your nervous system, and you often hide behind psychosomatic maladies to avoid making decisions that are critical. Continuous emotional disturbances can take their toll on your kidneys, which happen to be the most vulnerable area of your body.

Justice becomes an obsession with you when anything unfair disturbs you. You want to make peace whenever possible and are often cast in the role of a mediator where there is conflict. Some of you are so fanatical in your desire to maintain harmony in all relationships that you can stretch the truth a little. You may have an inclination to run from a situation since you find arguing too unsettling and disagreeable.

Like the Virgo native, you have a tendency to be very critical of others, and it is perhaps for this very reason that you often cling to one partner and do not make the close friendships that you need or desire. At times of stress you may be tempted to form a dependency on drugs or alcohol, which ultimately brings on ill health.

As a general rule you enjoy good health, but you are prone to continual colds, sniffles, and stuffy sinus conditions. Your kidneys, bladder, and lower back are also susceptible.

Foods you need to eat are mushrooms, brown rice, fish, eggs, greens, figs, citrus fruits, carrots, watercress, spinach, peas, celery, beets, apples, almonds, wheat and wheat germ, dates, poultry, asparagus, chamomile (soothing for restless and indecisive temperaments), and raisins. You must guard against the tendency to indulge in rich foods. Supplement your diet with vitamins A and E and iodine (found in fish and seafoods, ocean kelp, radishes, and squash). Your daily intake of copper—found in radishes, oysters, cucumbers, and lettuce—should also be given attention. Herbs helpful to you are thyme, watercress, rosemary, rose hips, parsley, and wintergreen. The vitamins and minerals you need are A, B complex, C, E, calcium, choline, copper, lecithin, iodine, magnesium, manganese, potassium, phosphorus, sodium, selenium, and zinc.

- You should cultivate self-confidence, independence, and an increased ability to face facts.
- You should avoid indecision, jealousy, and your compulsive need to balance everything.
- Companions harmonious with your sign are Capricorn, Aries, Cancer, Leo, and Sagittarius.

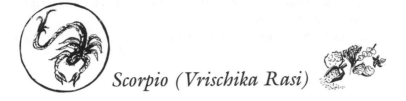

Scorpio (Vrischika Rasi)

You are a Scorpio (Scorpion) if you were born between October 23 and November 21. Pluto is your planetary ruler. Some astrologers believe that, as for Aries, Mars is your second planetary ruler. Your opposite and complementary sign is Taurus. You are a fixed water sign, which means you must express yourself intuitively. The most visible feature of your sign is its ability to transform, re-form, and regenerate values and things—in other words, spiritual transformation. Pluto, your ruling planet, has a purifying and cathartic effect in your life as you are always secretly experiencing metamorphic changes.

You are extremely intense, determined, and passionate about everything you do. As a water sign you are involved with other people, empathize with them, and therefore have the capacity to enrich their lives. You are very sensitive and easily hurt by other people's opinions of you. Like Cancer natives, you conceal your pain, and on the outside you are astonishingly cool, calm, and collected. As a matter of fact, you possess a great deal of personal power and great strength of purpose, courage, and perseverance. You are not an indecisive or ambivalent person and as such find it extremely difficult to compromise. You are shrewd and have a definite talent for summing up people and knowing exactly whom to trust. For you there is no middle ground; you either love or hate. Like your complementary and opposite sign, Taurus, you have a sensual nature, and jealousy and possessiveness are also traits of your sign. You can be unreasonably suspicious and can get very depressed.

Your wit can be biting and sarcastic like the sting of a Scorpion. You can be rather ruthless if you feel you have been exploited and deceived or if you find others are circum-

venting your plans. You can be a loyal and trusting friend
but a dangerous enemy if you are provoked.

Whether you are influenced by the lower or the higher
vibrations of your sign, you manifest a deep intensity that
results from the invisible and secret side of existence. You are
a very private person and take added precautions to guard
your privacy. You are profoundly interested in the occult
sciences and the mysteries of life and death. You have a
natural ability to uncover and see through other people's
secrets. Like your opposite sign, Taurus, you love to be
around nature and benefit enormously from being there.

Your tendency to keep your problems to yourself over a
period of time could manifest itself in physical ailments. You
should make a concerted effort to trust and confide in your
friends instead of being suspicious of them. The toxins
released into your bloodstream by your harboring suspicion
and revenge can take its toll on your health. Because of your
intensity, mental relaxation and rest are vital for you if you
are to remain healthy.

Your physical body is susceptible in the areas of the
sexual organs, the muscular and excretory systems, repro-
ductive organs, kidneys, and bladder. You tend to suffer
from disorders and diseases pertaining to these organs,
including constipation, painful menstruation, and hernia.
You have a tendency to catch infections easily, especially
those of the nose and throat.

You should eat plenty of fresh vegetables and fruits and
should avoid a diet that is too rich in fats or that contains
stimulants. A low-fat diet can help you keep your weight
down, something natives of your sign find difficult to maintain in the later years. Your high-protein diet should include
lean meat, seafood, poultry, eggs, yogurt, nuts, and soybeans.

You need to eat foods such as prunes, brewer's yeast,
parsley, peaches, cauliflower, lemons, onions, garlic, cauliflower, leeks, turnips, radishes, figs, raspberries, strawberries, asparagus, kale, and black cherry and chamomile tea
(soothing for restless temperaments). Herbs helpful to you
are garlic, ginger, onion, peppermint, horseradish, kelp,

watercress, and rosemary. The vitamins and minerals you need are A, B_2, B_{12}, B complex, C, D, E, K, iron, selenium, phosphorus, vanadium, sodium, and zinc.

- You should cultivate a spirit of forgiveness and better social adjustment.
- You should avoid secrecy, jealousy, excesses, willfulness, possessiveness, and revenge.
- Companions harmonious with your sign are Aquarius, Pisces, Taurus, Cancer, and Leo.

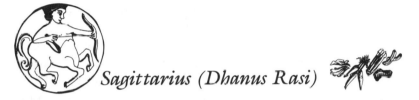 *Sagittarius (Dhanus Rasi)*

You are a Sagittarius (Archer) if you were born between November 22 and December 21. Your ruling planet is Jupiter. Your opposite and complementary sign is Gemini. You are a mutable fire sign, which means you are versatile, sensitive, intelligent, nervous, and very curious about life.

By nature you are an idealist, straightforward, optimistic, adventurous, and altruistic. Your approach to life is earnest and open. You are broad-minded and tolerant, and you set high standards for yourself. You trust people and expect others to do the same. You are imaginative, dependable, friendly, and easygoing. Your judgment is swift. You have the attitude of a philosopher, and unlike some other signs, you do not take life seriously. Jupiter, your ruling planet, associated with good fortune and expansiveness, often gives you a happy life with a great deal of fortune. You are extremely proud of your ancestry, your friends, your country, and your talents, and you are disagreeable and disenchanted when they deceive you.

You are a traveler and constantly want to be journeying. You enjoy the outdoor life and are less fiery than the other two fire signs—Aries and Leo. Like your complementary and opposite sign, Gemini, you cannot bear to be cooped up or tied down, and you want others to respect your need for freedom. If they do not, sooner or later your health will suffer. However, you need to be disciplined and cultivate patience. In your overexpansive frame of mind you tend to gamble and take unnecessary chances that leave you frustrated when your ideas or your speculative ventures do not materialize. You do need to be practical. You have a tendency to be unreliable because you cannot complete one task before going on to another, nor can you be tied down to any firm commitment. Boredom is your greatest enemy, often causing mental tiredness, and you need the motivation of a challenge. You have interests in a wide number of subjects (often in a rather pseudo-intellectual way), but you are capable of deep contemplation and can become completely absorbed in anything that really interests you. The various forms of nervous and circulatory disorders that afflict you often have a psychogenic (caused by mental conflicts) origin.

Cruelty of any kind is foreign to your nature, and you will go to great lengths to avoid hurting others. Ironically, your direct approach to everything, including human relationships, often results in your being tactless and sometimes offending people. Marriage for you can be and is a disenchanting experience, unless you find someone who is sympathetic to your deep-felt need for personal freedom. You want your companion to have faith in you, not to distrust you. For this reason alone, you cannot bear any sort of family dissension, jealousy, or confinement for very long.

As a native of Sagittarius, you must heed a word of caution. You are by nature accident-prone and are advised against any impulsive tendencies and reckless sport, which can be destructive to you. When injuries do occur, they usually involve the pelvis, legs, sacral bones, buttocks, and muscles of the hips and thighs. Your body is susceptible in the areas of the liver, hips, legs, thighs, tissues, and the pituitary gland. As a rule you enjoy good health unless you indiscriminately weaken it through overindulgence in alcohol, dietary indiscretions, or intemperance.

You simply must exercise self-restraint in the consumption of rich foods. To make sure your liver is functioning in a healthy manner, you should take C and B-complex vitamins, especially choline (also found in wheat germ, calf's liver, egg yolks, and soybeans).

Foods you need to eat are carrots, greens, rice bran, parsnips, cucumbers, green leafy vegetables, pumpkin seeds, egg yolks, asparagus, peas, okra, liver, bran, and oats. Herbs helpful to you are bay leaf, sage, parsley, peppermint, fennel, thyme, rosemary, fenugreek, marjoram, and dandelion. The vitamins and minerals you need are A, B_{13}, B_{15}, B complex, C, E, choline, phosphorus, sulfur, and zinc.

- You should cultivate tact, self-discipline, and perseverance.
- You should avoid reckless sport, overbearing attitudes, impulsive tendencies, and boasting.
- Companions harmonious with your sign are Pisces, Aries, Gemini, Leo, and Virgo.

Capricorn (Makara Rasi)

You are a Capricorn (Goat) if you were born between December 22 and January 20. Saturn (responsibility and practicality) is your natural planetary ruler, which means you are given responsibilities whether you like it or not and cannot afford to ignore them without dire consequences. Your opposite and complementary sign is Cancer. You are a cardinal earth sign, which means ambition, activity, tremendous stress, and remarkable achievement. Like the other earth signs, Taurus and Virgo, you are stable, patient, and reliable, and you believe in keeping your feet firmly on the ground.

You are industrious, conservative, thrifty, methodical, and cautious. You are security-minded. Your material, social,

and spiritual values are based on stable and enduring struc-
tures. You are somewhat reserved, creating a wall between
yourself and others. Your sign represents big industrial and
commercial enterprises. You are very ambitious and are
willing to work and wait for results. Your caution along with
your perseverance and strong determination help you realize
your ambitions all the way to the top. Your ambition is,
however, for power rather than for edification and glory.
Even if you amass a fortune, you are often inclined to be
frugal, and you are obsessed with amassing material possessions. Like your opposite sign, Cancer, you appreciate a
happy home life and provide for your family, taking your
duties and responsibilities very seriously.

You are to some extent self-centered, and you can be
pessimistic, melancholic, and limited in your outlook. You
can be unforgiving and can hold a grudge. Resentments held
over long periods of time do have neurotic consequences.
Your underlying weakness results from being indifferent to
people with emotional needs. You can be overcritical. You
have a tendency to be overconscientious and rigid. An un-
yielding mind is frequently found in an inflexible body. Your
general health can be affected unfavorably because of your
emotional inhibitions. You should develop flexibility and
tolerance. You victimize yourself because of your unfounded
fears and anxieties, thereby increasing the adrenaline in your
blood.

Capricorn rules the knees, shins, bones, teeth, skin,
and skeletal system. Your most frequent accidents involve
broken bones, bruises, sprains, dislocations, and knee injuries. You can live to a ripe old age if you exercise common
sense regarding your health. The best tonic for good health
is laughter. Don't take yourself so seriously; start to look at
the lighter and brighter side of life.

When illness does attack you, it can be chronic, and you
tend to brood over your ailments and become despondent,
convincing yourself that your condition is hopeless. This
finally becomes a self-fulfilling prophecy. Circulation of the
blood through the tissues becomes sluggish; elimination

can be restricted so that toxins and waste matter build up in your body.

Exercise care in your eating habits and avoid meat rich in fat, greasy foods, rich sauces and gravies, and alcohol. Your daily diet should include sufficient amounts of protein foods such as lean meat, yogurt, cottage cheese, eggs, and legumes. You should try to drink plenty of water between meals.

Other foods you need to eat are carrots, red beets, broccoli, citrus fruits, tomatoes, parsley, seaweed, yams, and liver. Herbs helpful to you are parsley, horseradish, and watercress. The vitamins and minerals you need are A, B_6, B_{12}, C, D, E, calcium, chlorine, fluorine, folic acid, iron, magnesium, manganese, potassium, phosphorus, selenium, sulfur, and zinc.

- You should cultivate an optimistic outlook, greater freedom of expression, taking yourself less seriously, and trust.
- You should avoid negativity, selfishness, and melancholy.
- Companions harmonious with your sign are Aries, Taurus, Cancer, Virgo, and Libra.

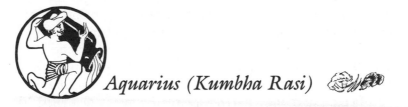

Aquarius (Kumbha Rasi)

You are an Aquarius (Water Bearer) if you were born between January 21 and February 19. Your planetary ruler is Uranus (one of the strongest planets, despite its great distance from the Earth). Some astrologers believe the planet Saturn to be your coruler. Your opposite and complementary sign is Leo. You are a fixed air sign, which means you must express yourself intuitively.

You are interested in the world of ideas and reason. The

influence of Uranus makes you unconventional, inventive, creative, and drawn to unusual subjects. You are extremely intelligent, and you are a great humanitarian. You have an innate sense of universal brotherhood and treat all of your friends with the same courtesy and somewhat impersonal hospitality. You gain an enormous sense of accomplishment and satisfaction from working with organizations and groups dedicated to the pursuit of helping others. You have a strange and tranquilizing effect on people who are emotionally agitated and needy.

You are a restless person with a great desire to change everything. You are optimistic, tolerant, open-minded, and always interested in new knowledge. You are often attracted to scientific and inventive work, and many of you are also found in the world of television. Your mind is penetrating, and your power of concentration is formidable. Once you have made up your mind to embark on a certain course of action, you are capable of great industry and strength of purpose. You are, however, a dreamer and can be unrealistic. You have a fascinating personality, and together with your originality, inventiveness, and freedom of thought, you often appear eccentric.

You are honest and dependable, yet like the other air signs, you have difficulty expressing your feelings. You seem to think that uncovering yourself to others not only makes you vulnerable but also is an invasion of your privacy. On the surface, however, you are an extremely friendly and sociable person. Your circle of friends ranges from the prosperous and famous to the poverty-stricken and infamous. You need a marriage partner or mate who is detached like you. You are loyal and faithful once a partnership is formed but cannot cope with your partner's possessiveness. Your undemonstrative nature could lead you to unhappy or emotionally unrewarding liaisons, which take their toll on your hypersensitive psyche, often resulting in various psychosomatic ailments. The most common of these are nervous disorders, neuralgia, and kidney disorders.

You maintain your own opinions in the face of all opposition. If you do not cultivate discipline, psychological difficulties can arise, affecting your physical well-being. Confining situations are incompatible with your desire for freedom.

Your temperament is often hard for your friends and family to understand. You frequently experience spells of seeming indifference, moodiness, and pessimism, which can undermine your general health. You are more sensitive than the natives of other signs to the changes of planetary configuration and as a result may experience inexplicable psychic disturbances. You are very susceptible to mental suggestions. Some of you sometimes suffer from strange and uncommon ailments of mysterious origin, which are hard for conventional medical practitioners to diagnose and treat.

Aquarius rules the circulatory system, calves, shins, and ankles. Some of you may suffer from varicose veins, swollen ankles, and muscular cramps. Normally you possess good health, but there is the constant need to cleanse the blood with proper diet supported by vitamins and minerals. When you do get ill, it is often quite sudden and may be brought about by abnormal habits and discord you have permitted to accumulate as a result of emotional inhibitions and by pushing yourself to the brink of human physical endurance. Unless you take measures now to prevent your health problems, during your mature years you are likely to develop high blood pressure and hardening of the arteries. Apart from following a low-fat diet, one of the most practical and comfortable ways to have a healthy cardiovascular system is to engage in regular exercise outdoors. Natives of your sign are not eager about exercise for the sake of health, but it is vital to keep you fit. If you follow a regular program of daily exercise, you will not experience leg cramps. Walking in the open air, doing stretching exercises, and doing daily deep-breathing yoga exercises will do wonders for you.

Because of poor circulation, your diet should be supplemented with vitamin C and bioflavonoids. Vitamin E is also beneficial in the prevention of vascular troubles, especially after the age of 35. You should eat fresh fruits such as oranges, lemons, apples, pears, grapes, and pineapple every day. Lack of calcium causes tension, irritability, and fatigue. Milk, hard cheese, mustard and turnip greens, soybeans, blackstrap molasses, and almonds are calcium-rich foods.

Generally, foods hold an insignificant place in your life. The foods you need to eat are broccoli, beans, spinach, fish, cheese, honey, lemons, apples, and turnip greens. Herbs helpful to you are comfrey, horseradish, cayenne, garlic, caraway, and rosemary. The vitamins and minerals your body needs are B_{12}, B_{15}, C, E, F, K, P, choline, folic acid, calcium, inositol, niacin, chromium, iron, potassium, selenium, vanadium, and zinc.

- You should cultivate freedom of the spirit, your intuitive powers, concern for the individual, and a better relation to practical things.
- You should avoid anarchy, disorder, fatigue, erratic habits, procrastination, and being scatterbrained.
- Companions harmonious with your sign are Taurus, Gemini, Leo, Libra, and Scorpio.

Pisces (Mina Rasi)

You are a Pisces (Two Fish, swimming in opposite directions) if you were born between February 20 and March 20. You are ruled by Neptune, the mysterious planet of illusion, delusion, deception and self-deception, imagination, idealism, glamor, decay, and extrasensory perception. Some astrologers believe that the planet Jupiter is coruler of your sign. Your opposite or complementary sign is Virgo. You are a mutable water sign, which means you use reason, serve others, make judgments, and determine what sacrifices and final adjustments have to be made.

You are sympathetic, artistic, passive, receptive, self-sacrificing, indecisive, inspiring, highly sensitive, and emotional. The planet Jupiter, your coruler, further emphasizes the expansiveness of your mind and spirit, qualities of benevolence, wisdom, and spontaneity. The desire to absorb experience empowers you to understand, transform, and overcome emotional suffering. Those of you who respond to the lower vibrations of your sign often stray through life, escaping through drugs and alcohol and gradually sinking into self-destruction until death frees your spirit from the chaos of your physical existence. You are very adaptable. Self-deception is common, and so is the deliberate deception of others if it will make life easier for you. Your way of avoiding disagreeable situations is to run from them, and this is why some of you turn to drugs and alcohol for solace. On the other hand, some of you, with your ultra-sensitivity, realize the danger of this kind of addiction and stay far away from it. You have a rare sense of artistic rhythm and are very susceptible to beauty. Acting appeals to you as it allows you to retreat into a world of make-believe.

You have an overwhelming need to feel loved and want to please everyone. You become very disillusioned if the comfort of being loved is not present. Disapproval and unkindness from others devastate you. However, your need for privacy is great as you can become mentally and emotionally drained by people.

You can become restless and vacillating in your affairs of the heart. In love you are devoted and tender, often assuming a passive role in the relationship. Owing to the tremendous impact your emotional life has on your general health, you should be careful about marrying a mate whose planetary positions are not in harmony with yours. Both men and women of your sign possess a strong sex drive, and some women of this sign choose a mate for sexual attraction. Since Pisces men are physically desirable, they do not have to be aggressive. Certain women seem to gravitate to them like magnets.

Some of you can be prone to prolonged emotional conflicts and for your own sake should seek the help of a competent psychiatrist as you do respond well to psychoanalysis. Your health problems are frequently emotionally induced conditions rather than stemming from exposure to germs and other external factors. At times, although you appear calm, collected, and relaxed, you may be shaking with anxiety. Such conditions have adverse effects on the functioning of your endocrine system, thereby paving the way for those ailments to which you are susceptible. You have a tendency to be pessimistic when you get ill. Pisces rules the feet, the duodenum, the body's fluids, the pituitary and pineal glands, and the lymphatic system and fibrin of the blood. Some of you tend to be overweight chiefly because you retain water. You may also suffer from swollen glands, nervous stress, and drug allergies. Some of you could be prone to drug or alcohol poisoning, to fish poisoning, and to water containing impurities. Because Pisces is a water sign, baths and swimming are an essential part of your recuperation from mental, physical, and emotional problems.

You require a high-protein diet rich in lean meat, eggs, seafood, cheese, yogurt, and nuts. You also need to eat foods such as raisins, dates, cereals, figs, molasses, beef liver, cucumbers, lima beans, almonds, lettuce, radishes, strawberries, lentils, onions, and barley. Herbs you need are kelp, arrowroot, horseradish, seaweed, and borage. Vitamins and minerals you need are A, B_{12}, B complex, C, E, folic acid, PABA, calcium, chromium, cobalt, copper, iodine, iron, and molybdenum.

- You should cultivate willpower, closer contact with reality, objectivity in judgments, directness, and warmth.
- You should avoid habit-forming drugs and alcohol, self-indulgence, and self-deception.
- Companions harmonious with your sign are Gemini, Cancer, Virgo, Scorpio, and Sagittarius.

Index